CONCEPT DESIGN 2

WORKS FROM SEVEN LOS ANGELES ENTERTAINMENT DESIGNERS
AND SEVENTEEN GUEST DESIGNERS

H.BELKER

S.BURG

J.CLYNE

M.GOERNER

N.PAGE

N.PUGH

S.ROBERTSON

+ guest artists :

NICOLAS BOUVIER

RYAN CHURCH

DYLAN COLE

KASRA FARAHANI

SEAN HARGREAVES

KHANG LE

WARREN MANSER

STEPHAN MARTINIERE

ED NATIVIDAD

RICK O'BRIEN

DAN QUARNSTROM

CHRISTIAN L. SCHEURER

OLIVER SCHOLL

FARZAD VARAHRAMYAN

MIKE YAMADA

FELIX YOON

FENG ZHU

TITAN BOOKS

DEDICATION

For all of you who were inspired by *Concept Design 1...*

Published by Titan Books
in association with Design Studio Press
A division of Titan Publishing Group Ltd
144 Southwark Street
London SE1 0UP
visit our website: **www.titanbooks.com**

Art Direction: Scott Robertson
Layout Production: Marsha Stevenson
Graphic design by Fancy Graphics
Web site: www.fancygraphics.net
Text Editor: Anna Skinner

Printed in China
First UK Edition May 2006

10 9 8 7 6 5 4 3 2

ISBN 1 84576 285 1

A CIP catalogue record for this title is available from
the British Library.

Porsche 911 is a registered trademark of
Dr. Ing. h.c. F. Porsche AG.
Corvette is a registered trademark of
General Motors Corporation.

CONTENTS

"Man is a genius when he is dreaming." Akira Kurosawa

Film is frequently talked about as art.
In such conversations, correlations are often made to the creative process of more "traditional" arts. Yet, such correlations do not exist. The personal control of the traditional arts does not exist. Uninhibited evolution of the concept from the first seminal spark to the completed artwork does not exist. Even the role of artist as sole determining creator and owner of the artwork does not exist.

Instead, it is the marketplace that influences every step of that creative process. Studios—the "patrons" of this art form—are banks, making investments in the business of entertainment. They acquire properties, rights, and talent at as low a price as possible and then market and sell them for whatever profit they can. No studio executive gets up and says, "Let's make some art today." It is a production line, ROI business. The film business as we know it is largely a craft—a simultaneous, collaborative process ultimately and strictly defined by commercial, not aesthetic, parameters.

I've wondered why some of the brilliantly talented artists I've met take part in this enterprise. They do it, we do it, because the pull of the Work is strong: an artist surrenders to its will, devoting themselves totally to its realization. You become the servant of the Work, Art's acolyte. It is often said that film is the dreaming of mankind, the most powerful medium in our culture for evoking the spirit world of the Imagination. Like dreams, there is only light shining in darkness, the luminous incarnation of a carefully crafted reality.

This book recognizes and celebrates concept artists, the magnificent dream hunters who, before any projector is switched on, ignite the first illuminating spark. Concept design is aspiration personified, the revered vocation of passionate idealists, courageous adventurers hungry to dwell in undiscovered countries.

Concept designers make the unknown knowable and animate. They render dreams and desires real and tangible. They speak the fluid language of Image, fashioning and manipulating the symbols and icons of our collective dreaming, and in doing so, give shape to unknown lands, life to unformed characters, and purpose to unimagined objects.

Finally, like all good parents, concept designers embrace the process of creation and surrender. They know only a fraction of their work may ever make it to the screen and even then they will most probably be anonymous. But even working invisibly, they KNOW what they have done. There is deep satisfaction in a gift expressed and shared with the world. As with all great artists, their work shines on forever, touching minds and hearts – light dancing in the dark – for generations to come.

Robert Gould
President, Imaginosis
a Transmedia Arts Company

INTRODUCTION

So here it is, the second volume of *Concept Design*. Before you jump into this new offering, I'd like to share a few thoughts on the time that has passed since the printing of *Concept Design 1*. First of all, thanks to those of you who helped make *Concept Design 2* a reality with your support and enthusiasm for the first book. As long as there is an interest we will continue this series. I am very happy with the quality of work in this edition of the series, and I feel that both the designers from the first book, and the new additions to our guest designer section, have really stepped up the work's quality and diversity.

When we started thinking about *Concept Design 2*, after we all recovered from completing the first book, we thought it would be really fun to invite a few more peers to join in the creation of this edition. Each of the guys featured in *Concept Design 1* invited some of their friends to join in our every-other-month meetings here at the studio. During these very inspiring get-togethers, we would share pieces in development for the book and do a little networking at the same time. Now that the book is finished, we are going to try to maintain these meetings so that we can continue talking about ideas and focus on *Concept Design 3*, which will begin development in 2006.

A few points on how this edition is organized. For this second volume of the series, you will first find ten spreads from each of the designers featured in *Concept Design 1*, followed by one spread each from our talented guest designers. All of the bios are now at the back of the book where you will also find contact information for the artists.

Design Studio Press has partnered with The Gnomon Workshop to create educational DVDs on concept art. Some of the pieces in this book were recorded as the subjects of those DVDs, available for purchase at www.thegnomonworkshop.com. Of the 24 designers featured in *Concept Design 2*, ten of them have created 39 educational DVDs to date on design, drawing and painting. If you are at all interested in learning more about how the work in this book was created, please look them up.

I want to thank the families of the talented concept artists featured in this book for allowing them the time, and giving them the support, to keep this book series alive. A special thanks, of course, to my comrades for wanting to be a part of *Concept Design 2*. To the regulars–Nick, Neville, Harald, James, Steve, and Mark–thanks again for busting your asses to move the bar up one more notch–nicely done. To the new guys–Khang, Mike, Felix, Christian, Oliver, Ryan, Feng, Stephan, Kasra, Farzad, Rick, Dan, Sean, Sparth, Dylan, Warren, and Ed–welcome aboard and thanks for making this book a special experience. I think that about covers it from my end; the rest is up to you. Enjoy the work, and we hope it inspires you to go out and create something special of your own.

All the best,
Scott Robertson
Los Angeles
Spring 2005

MARK GOERNER

NICK PUGH

SCOTT ROBERTSON

JAMES CLYNE

STEVE BURG

NEVILLE PAGE

HARALD BELKER

This section of *Concept Design 2* features work from the original seven designers from *Concept Design 1*. The order of each designer's work is organized according to the text block on the right. Again, a special thanks to them for their successful efforts. Enjoy.

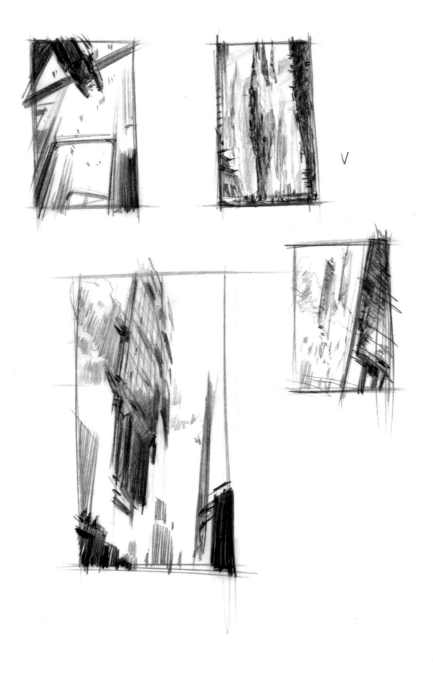

REEF CITY

MARK GOERNER:

In the low powerful resonant hum of the city center, there lies a fine lace of cackles and bickering from its occupants. The sound of shifting wares and large infrastructural machines churn out an industrial rhythm, a bass line for a digital choir broadcasting millions of signals in a stream of discord from every nook and alley. Like weighted fish, the dwellers swim in their respective planes, performing the task of defending their transparent territories. The soul of the city is built from a grid of hovering totems set forth by the elders as if it were a medley of sticks in a tub of brine. As time creeps forward, the buildings' facets swell outward in accordance with its urban demands and the vehicular pathways that swim through its voids.

As a newcomer arrives to make his way through these guarded fortresses of commerce, a shifting of focus pulls the darkest grain out for the take.

MARK GOERNER: SIR REGINALD THE 7TH OF FREINZSCHWAUDLE

As the direct descendant of Reginald the first of Squirthborough, the highly powerful magnum of the kelp quarries in the early kingdom of MupftKriest, and first son of Bruce of Fureigh, Reginald the 7th found his path of fortune through entirely different means. His was the pursuit of great adventure, establishment of colonies in distant oceans, and inventions created and utilized to secure these new territories for the kingdom's investors. For example, the Hydroquafulator was a complex device, which became the primary tool of choice by Jorvlic sailors for extracting the equally rare and valuable Quince from their calcified shells.

Reginald's passion for innovation was not isolated to tools of harvest; he also helped create the new metric, which enabled Gyrotahinnian navigation to function effectively. This allowed not only his crew but also numerous other explorers and vagabonds to extend into the uncharted seas beyond the treacherous atolls of Trouzer. As an avid collector of oddities and keepsakes from his many conquests, Reginald was most known for his love of nature and anthropology. One of the capital's favorite dishes, in fact, is named after Reginald and features the Noflato, a tangy bean with a rich inner meat that he discovered on the distant shores of Schuhm while tracking the endangered Pufu.

In his later years, Reginald established and served as chancellor of the famous Freinzschwaudle Institute of Oceanic Studies and Warfare, where he often spoke on discovery and seamanship. Although he was serious about education and love of country, his softer side will most likely be remembered. His concern for the community was shown through generous contributions to the underprivileged by founding the Children's Amphibious Urban League, as well as erecting the Reginald Theater of Aquatic Arts, where, to this day, the Festival of Tides is celebrated in honor of his prowess as a pioneer, visionary, and most importantly for Freinzschwaudle's signature dish, Reginald bean pie.

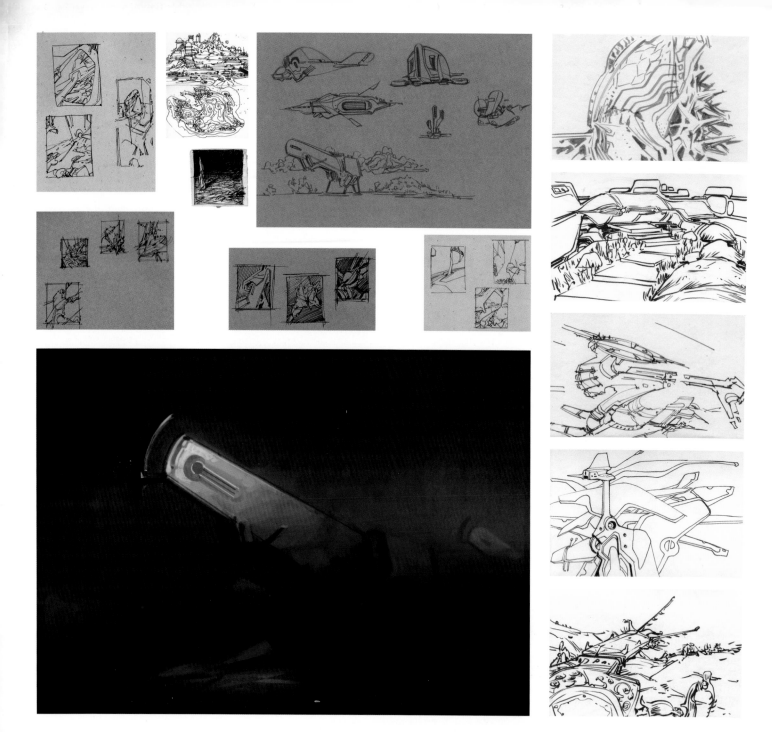

MARK GOERNER:

PILE O' FODDER

This smattering of sketches and rough illustrations show a bit of the miscellaneous mental and gestural rants I make in the in-between times, usually in bars with poor lighting and a penchant for oddly named drinks. Some of these directions turned into paintings in this book, while others serve as design exploration for what I think of as sketch-personality affirmation. I tend to lean toward the toned and grainy papers when sketching. As with shoes and teeth, pure white can be a frightening thing.

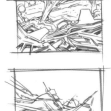

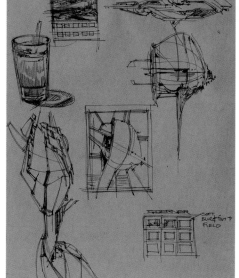

MARK GOERNER:

GIGABOCCE

In a cavernous arena large enough to contain a small moon, there is sport of epic power in the last stages of game play. It is a competition that brings all neighboring provinces together to match the wit of their technicians and the strength of their technology. From the staging precipices located in the upper quadrants of the gigantic dome, contenders ready the slave carriers to launch and deliver devastating blows to the obstacles and opponent's markers below. Passes are made to sweep in and dislodge strategic placements of markers in order to secure key locations. As pieces crash down with pulverizing force, teams analyze and put in motion new actions to better their score. Due to the highly complex nature of the obstacles and their unknown makeup, machine computation in strategy gives way to intuition of the controllers. From mezzanines around the perimeter of the arena as well as remote locations, audiences observe all conceived angles via swarms of cameras that trace and dive through the melee. As the pieces land and fill the final zones, remaining time is shown by lit halos that define the success of the strongest teams. In these last riotous moments, a flurry of pieces is lobbed in the attempt to sway the outcome.

In starting this illustration, there was little narrative, just an interest in tinting the composition and articulating the abstract forms of the sketch. I saw right off a cold and neutral color palette with some surfaces potentially lost in the tone of the background. It was in the final stages of detailing the design, balancing colors, and honing the surface finish that I saw the abstraction give way to a more specific story. I wanted to aid in the scale and put in some redundancy, so I added the other distant yet similar silhouettes as the foreground. This helped to define the foreground object a bit better and give depth to the flat haze. The bands of lighting were intensified to provide form to the unseen space behind the haze and to concentrate the eye toward the center.

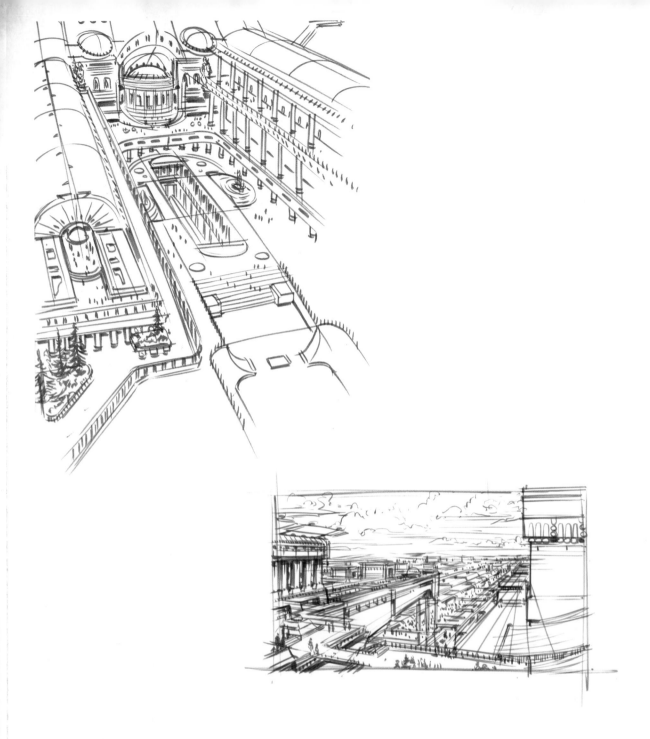

NEO ROME

MARK GOERNER:

A chorus of echoing horns fades into the roar from a terraced ocean of crowds in the midst of a massive ceremony. Kings perched as gods oversee the empire in full glory while below its citizens celebrate their civic allegiance, filling the main promenade in a collective flow toward the central square. Dirigibles float overhead, documenting the activities and shuttling dignitaries into the heart of the parade. The main event that showcases the year's bounty, conquests, and innovations is about to begin after which an all-night festival will charge and illuminate the city's living grid.

As a wee kid, the grand empires of the B.C. era sparked my interest to the point where I considered archeology a serious career goal, along with being a professional spy and space traveler. It was the scale of those civic projects, the consummate sculptures, and underlying meridians aligning those cities that sank into my consciousness and inspired thoughts of city planning and architectural design. The spaces, defined by gigantic finely hewn stones and stagger-ing walls, had a warm, urban atmosphere that few buildings and domains in our modern landscape of hollow facades have been able to achieve. I would love to see the innovations in computer-controlled machining and design find their way into the manipulation of hybridized natural and engineered materials to create even greater scales than those of the historical kingdoms.

GRAND CENTRAL

MARK GOERNER:

These sketches and this illustration are the product of a DVD series on the designing and illustrating interior spaces with pens and markers and finalizing in a digital medium. The DVD follows the likely path I would use to create a specific environment and refine the color and tone after scanning in a chosen drawing. Even though most of my final work is digital, I still like the feeling of playing around on paper and having that aspect still in hand when searching for a design.

My goal, when starting this series, was to develop a large space with a strong, symmetrical centralized core flanked by mezzanines and a focal element at one end. After generating some varied plazas, rooms, and halls, I came upon the idea of an expansive train station as a likely direction. After the usual scan and transparent layer attribute change to the chosen sketch, I filled a backing layer with large swatches of airbrushed colors loosely related to a sample color palette I found online. Once the overall mood was struck, the layer-by-layer building of elements was developed, starting with the major lighting kiosks and background window glazing, followed by balconies, signage, catwalks, train windows, and secondary lighting fixtures. A common attribute to most of these layers for this particular piece was the process of creating an element, copying, pasting, scaling, and grouping with the previous in order to create the necessary repeat of elements. Additional atmosphere and detail was added in later steps to enhance the believability of the space.

MARK GOERNER:

HOUSE ALLUVIAL

This spread is devoted to the exploration of a logistical and aesthetic solution to a house design in the hills of coastal California. Although the reality of hard points, building codes, architectural review boards, and costs loom ever present over the project, I wanted to keep my focus at this early stage on the general philosophy of the space and its integration into the landscape. My interest in the house's form is a design that coincides with the natural sedimentary sandstone that is exposed and eroded around the local mountain ranges. The likeness to the fractures, tone, and staggered layers found in these formations would be reflected by swept, structural planes that are shifted and oriented to the views around the site. Penetrating verticals will help to define some of the more intimate spaces of the interior and support the horizontal roofing surfaces and pathways. I am also opting to reinstall some of the indigenous plants disrupted in the preparation and construction of the site back on top of the house's roof and surrounding footprint to aid in the continuous flow of color and local landscape over the site. The guiding principal driving the physical presence of the house is to fuse elements of directional automotive surfacing, the cavelike atmospheres of early monolithic construction, and elements of asymmetrical Asian gardens.

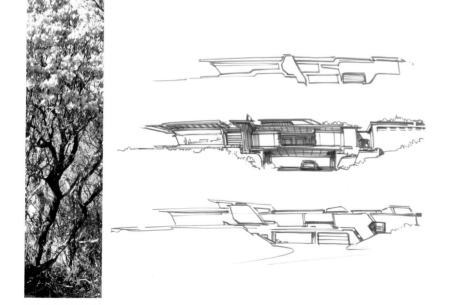

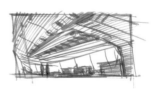

MARK GOERNER: # NOCTURNAL TRANSMISSION

In the sharp, frozen space of the upper atmosphere, hung with clouds, a transportation web circumnavigates the darkness. Like sap flowing in a giant Sequoia, containers holding bits of the world's goods move in vertical streams between ground and sky where they await a transfer to take them on their arced destination across the planet. Silent automated crafts continue the incremented flow in the night sky, while below a demanding society continues to devour and process.

This ditty, like a few of my other paintings in this book, was started from an abstract composition and form-driven sketch. I picked it out of my sketchbook for its odd, long tendril nature and canted position in frame. The feeling of tree-house isolation is what sparked the beginning of my color work to establish mood. I saw a purple-to-blue nocturnal with electric highlights striking corners and laying down a reflective track. Once the canvas was filled with a field of cobalt, and the silhouette of the subject was darkened, I

began dolloping in a cloud pattern, focusing the eye into a central space. Then I noodled the figure for a while in the block form at the top of the stem until the shapes and transitions felt right. Frustrated by a flatness issue, a pass at indicating an aerial landscape below and a moon behind, helped revive my enthusiasm and grounded the painting with some vague likeness of a discernible space. Lastly, I saw a pocket in the composition in need of balance, so I inserted the foreground craft. It was designed to trace the nature of the other floating techno blobs and aid once again in the depth of space. So what began as a purely abstract toiling ended in a narrative with unlikely objects in an equally unlikely, but recognizable, space.

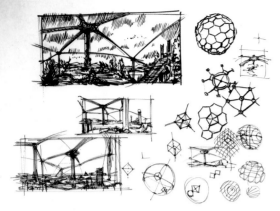

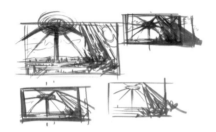

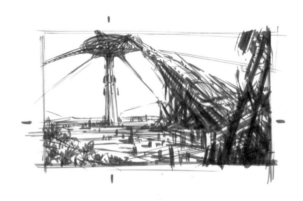

MARK GOERNER:

MOON CRASH 5, VERNAL REPRISE

This is a revisitation of the series I did in the last book and relates to the evolution of life and civilization on a planet whose surface was permanently altered after being bombarded by its own fractured moon.

This image picks up another thousand years after the last, at which point society has reached an apparent zenith of technology and expansion around its own planet. Except this time, another catastrophic event has rendered the dominant inhabitants seemingly extinct. Their once triumphant web that inscribed the planet has fallen ill in the wake of structural failure. The other species have crept from their recesses to regain territories lost, to coat and tarnish the once omnipresent civilization with their own brand of organic expression.

The scribbles above show the meandering I did to get to the large final piece. I started with a more descriptive illustration of the structures from the past series, resulting in an overly complex composition and incorrect space for the

goal I was after. After a few months of leaving it to rot in the ol' hard drive, I started from scratch and hit on the illusive composition I was after with a few brush pen doodles. I fused the two lower thumbnail sketches and did a quick, rough color pass that hit it squarely were I wanted it. The trick from that point out was to refine and texture while keeping the atmosphere and freshness unhampered.

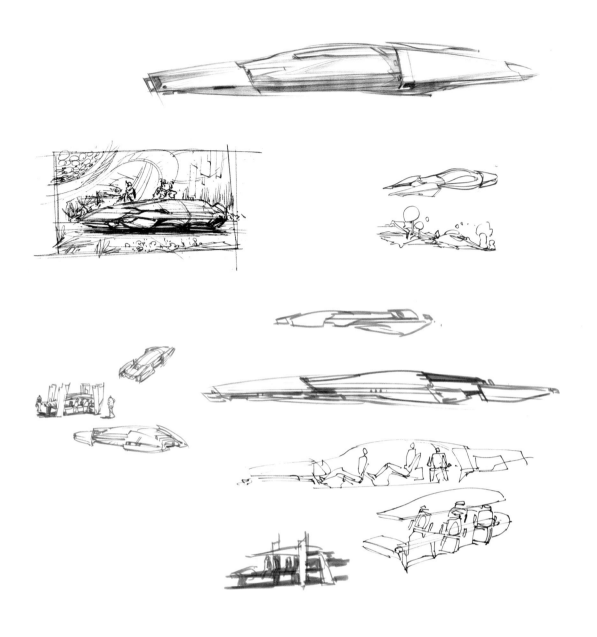

CRIMSON CRAFT

MARK GOERNER:

I couldn't leave this series without illustrating the much needed floating car. After all, what we need now, more than ever, is a high-speed airborne highway. Our cars and trucks elevated a few feet to perhaps miles above the pavement will solve so many of modern society's problems. Think of the thrill, the open space, the view, and the absence of tires; but most importantly, think of the children.

Unlike other spreads I have done here, the final image was purely digital without a sketch to work from. I was loosely playing with line, form, and odd color passes, with little interest in taking it to any finished level. After a bit of that, an atmosphere came to mind; specifically, a dank night in the city. I have always had a magical interest in cars in the rain, especially when the physics of movement applies. In refinement, I wanted to convey a transformable vehicle that fractures into winged legs, allowing for the floor to drop out of the way and the doors to open as a canopy outward. The idea being that entering the vehicle could be similar to saddling up to a cushioned swing set that would envelop you once you were ready to go.

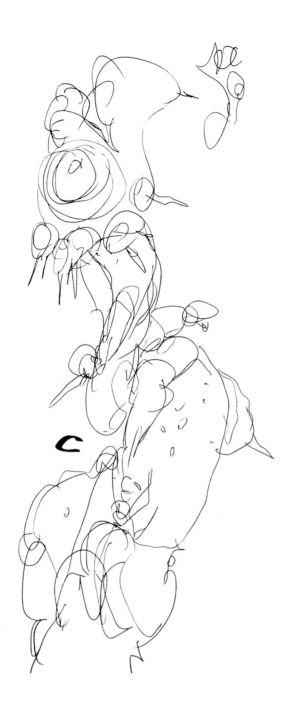

NICK PUGH:

TROPICAL CREATURE

In many respects, my ultimate goal in the design process is to come up with an original artistic language—a daunting task that can sometimes be achieved with labor and luck. Despite one's attempt to generate true originality, it is far more likely that the resulting art will be derivative of the influences that permeate the artist's brain. The work on the following pages represents my struggle with this goal. Some of the work can be seen in my DVD set on original artistic language. The line sketch on the far left is a select from about 200 pages of free-form, arm-waving-with-a-pen drawings. The shaded sketch shows developing form and volume to the line sketch, and the color image is the creature put into an environment with lighting and texture.

NICK PUGH:

BARNYARD

The art on this page is from a story that I created in collaboration with my friend, Bill Kroyer, called "Funny Farm." It is a tale of very genetically modified farm animals who escape their experimental factory-farm lab and find themselves among other normal animals. This character is a goat that can eat anything. His jaws and teeth are designed to act as a garbage disposal, and the nasal skull plate acts as a compression brace for chewing very hard substances.

NICK PUGH:

15 KINGSBURY

The painting here is a crazy version of my grandmother's house in Massachusetts. I did the sketch a few years ago and then used it in a plein aire hybrid technique where I painted the color part from life (photo above) over a scanned line drawing. It was a fun process where the live painting part was not of a real scene but of a made-up one with real world lighting applied from what I saw and felt standing there in the front yard. The design is inspired by my uncle Neil, who is a designer and contractor, and builds custom colonial homes in Boston's suburbs. I was fortunate enough to work for him, and this picture is a challenge to the possible shapes one could build while still maintaining a traditional aesthetic.

CREATURES

NICK PUGH:

I have always been fascinated by evolution and the "what if?" of its endless futuristic possible variations. These creatures are just fun explorations of this idea. The reptilian one is a descendant of a marine iguana. It has evolved a protective head plate and feeding apparatus for plankton. The babison is just that–a baboon/bison hybrid.

VEHICLES

NICK PUGH:

These vehicles are also from the DVD series on original artistic language. A form language can be applied to any number of different categories, ranging from creatures and environments to vehicles. It is fun to see how many subtle versions one can create. These vehicles are bubbling and billowing along in a sort of rhythmic motion. Soft and unclear, their shape and texture blend into the environment as they whisk their occupants along to their destinations.

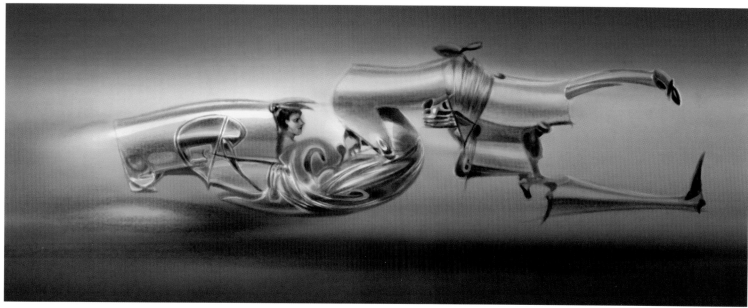

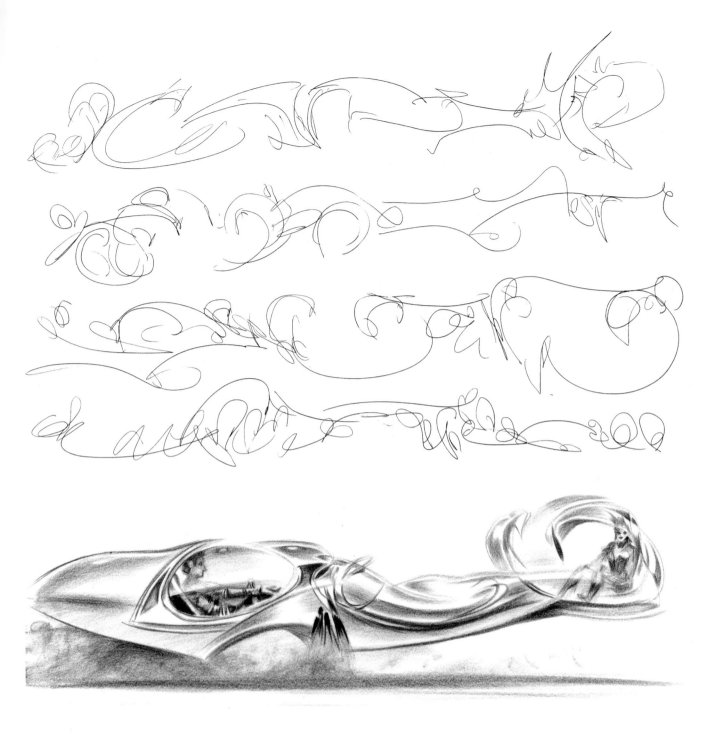

NICK PUGH:

VEHICLES

This is another liquid-vehicle exploration. I'm applying a curvilinear language to more literal architectural elements and integrating a super-shiny vehicle into it. It is an illustration of my continued fascination with a future where mechanical form takes on animated qualities; the rigid shell becomes soft and flexible.

DIGITAL PLEIN AIRE PAINTING

NICK PUGH:

These paintings are from a trip I took to Europe. I was in Germany for a car show in November 2003 and drove to Bilbao to see the Guggenheim museum. I drove through the Loire Valley in France and painted some pictures on my laptop along the way. The river was fun to paint with its reflections and nice lighting. On my return from Spain, I stopped on a rainy stretch of road south of Bordeaux, called Bassin, where there are rows and rows of tall pine trees in a giant farm that stretch for 150 kilometers or so. I had already painted one rear-view picture, and as I started another a small blue car spun past and flipped end over end, falling into a ditch (photo above). After checking on the woman in the car, (she was okay) I went back to my car and sketched what I had just seen. Wow, that was live digital painting!

NICK PUGH:

DIGITAL PLEIN AIRE PAINTING

More assorted live digital paintings. Many of these pictures are from a summer trip to New England. The lighting, weather, and relaxed environment are perfect for making art. I seem to be attracted to painting water or waterfront images. These sketches are just studies in lighting, color, and composition. The process of doing these pictures is a hybrid between traditional painting and digital photography. Your eyes and body are the lens and light capture, and the computer is the "film" and printing.

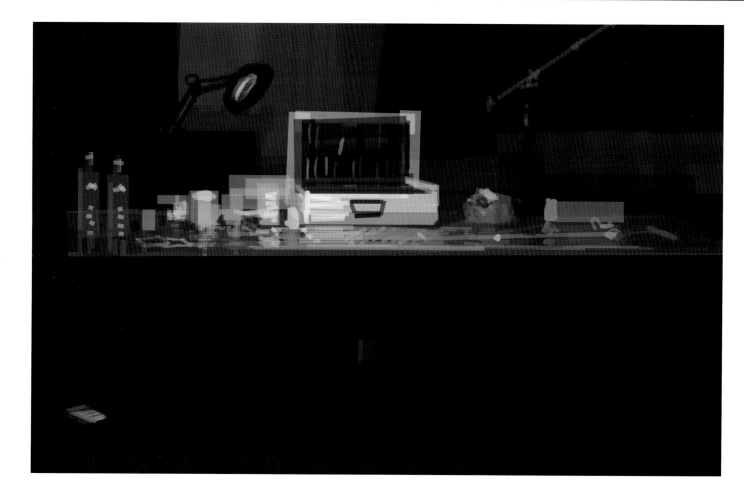

NICK PUGH:

DIGITAL PLEIN AIRE PAINTING

Autumn in New England has a reputation for great color, and this is for a reason. I was thrilled to be able to have my computer out in the woods during this time in 2003. The way the sun illuminates the leaves, the comfortable working conditions, and the incredible contrast of sky and foliage all make an environment perfect for creating art. It is such an exhilarating challenge to try to capture such strong, vivid color on the computer screen in these little paintings. The screen is so grey and flat when compared to the surrounding environment, but if the process succeeds the printed image has a close feeling to the original scene.

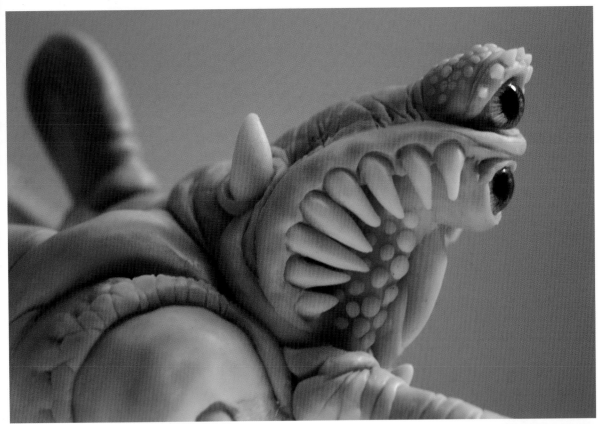

NICK PUGH:

SCULPTURE

The sculptures shown here were created for a Rhythm & Hues Siggraph booth. They were just an exercise in free-form creature design. The big one on the right is a birdlike thing that has evolved a way of skating on bony hooflike feet. It hunts seals, quietly sliding up to them as they come up for air, then scoops them out with its long hook-shaped claws. The others are some random creatures that might inhabit the same world.

SCOTT ROBERTSON:

This was a really fun piece to do because it came together so easily. The value sketch above was done first, by compositing some photographs I had taken of various things, none of which could be identified by the time I had collaged them together in Photoshop. I looked at the value collage for some time and found what I thought could be an interesting composition, then I went into roughing out the forms. Since I started with a value collage, I already had a hint of depth due to atmospheric perspective. I simply tried to find the shapes that were already in the piece. When I went to the color stage on the right, I fell back into one of my favorite color palettes, orange and blue. I love the look of late afternoon sun on rusted steel. You can see a lot of the first sketch remains in the finished piece. The little ship with the pilot in it on the crane was a fun challenge, rendering part of the ship in direct sunlight and the front shadow area illuminated by the artificial light coming from the crane above the nose of the ship. I'm most happy with the shapes of the

crane, which reflect an evolving, sculptural form language that I credit Mark and James for inspiring me to pursue. Working with value to explore various forms is a very fun way to paint and design. After I have chosen my light source creating new forms by simply changing values feels very similar to sculpting with clay. Everyone's brains work the same in that forms are perceived by value changes. Remembering this simple fact and then incorporating it into the painting and design process is a great way to work.

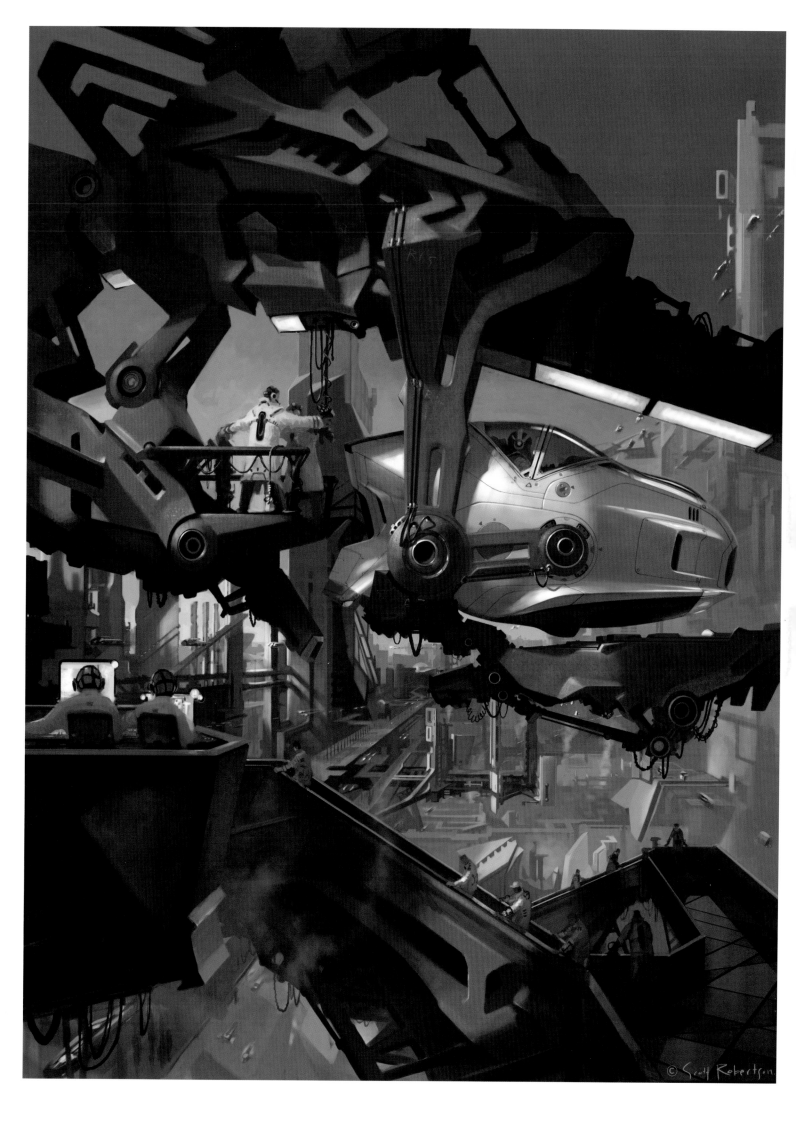

ANT SHIPS

Neville has a great book in our library full of black-and-white, microscopic photographs of ants. I started this spread of sketches by looking at those photos and trying to reassemble similar forms into the spacecraft or "antcraft" you see here. These are simple graphite sketches on basic layout paper. I find all sorts of design inspiration in nature. Insects make for easy translation into quirky flying vehicles since they are already a left-right, symmetrical hard-surface form. On the following page you will see that one of these sketches was the start for its color rendering, in which the ship rises through the clouds and heads into the upper atmosphere. In a lot of these designs, it is easy to recognize the ant's head or what might have been an eye at one time. When including something recognizable from the source material, I like to try to reverse the direction of things, like making the familiar ant's head the rear of the antcraft. Whenever I need a good boost of inspiration, I know I can always count on Mother Nature.

SCOTT ROBERTSON:

ASCENT, CHECK POINT 12

Above is the color rendering of one of the antcraft rising through the clouds on its ascent into space. If you look closely you can get a sense of the scale of this antcraft when you find the pilot's head in the cockpit. It's really fun to start the design of an immense building, or in this case a vehicle, from something so small. By simply playing with the scale of the human figure in relation to the object, you can completely change the viewer's first perception of what scale they might expect the forms to have. My favorite part of the piece is probably the cast shadow on the clouds and the subtle exhaust glow in the clouds below.

The piece to the right started life as one of my abstract marker-sketch collages in Photoshop. Slowly the rocks took shape, and I added the planet in the far distance to tie these two pieces together for this spread. I had been visiting a friend of mine in Vancouver, and I showed him a work in progress of this piece. He suggested that I add a foreground element to it to better guide the viewer's eye into

the background. Steven, I hope you like what I came up with because it's too late to change it now. The story I was thinking of that gave rise to the triangle element and the flight-line buoys is that they are part of some kind of flight-training obstacle course, if you will. Young pilots must maneuver their spacecraft at high speed through this tricky light-triangle without breaking the beam. The flight path is made more unpredictable by the unstable wind conditions, which can occur through the gap in the rocks.

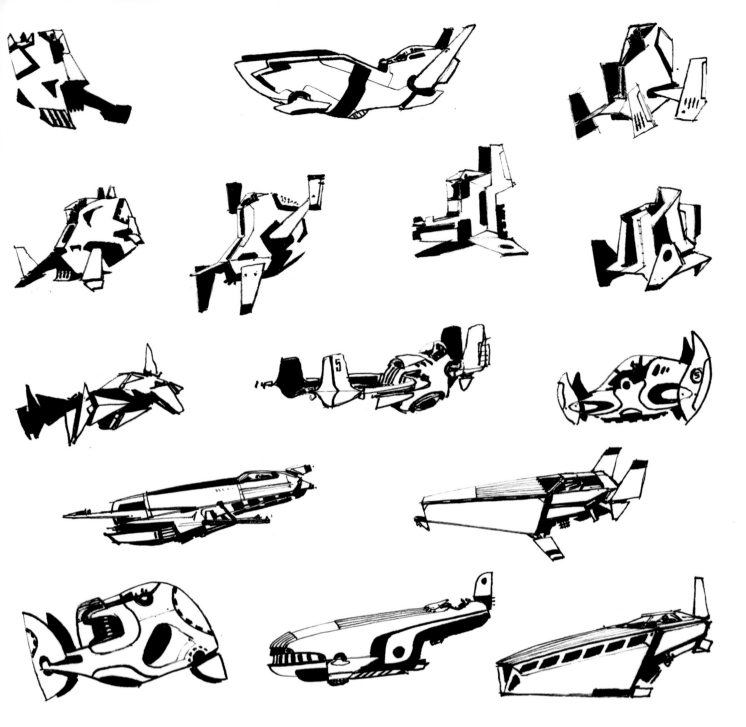

SCOTT ROBERTSON:

Sometime over the last year I started using a big chisel-tip calligraphy ink pen to draw these quick, little thumbnail sketches. The perspective ones are pretty loose but fast and fun to do. You can find a lot of these ship designs in my other color pieces. When I have a big environment to do and I need to populate it with a bunch of flying ships, I open up this file and grab the ones that will match the perspective and then drag them into the painting. I obviously love to sketch these little quirky ships. Each time I draw them I try to push the forms in new directions. They are fairly simple as you can see, and the primary objective is to explore interesting silhouettes, proportions, and graphics. I spend no time on surfacing the forms at this point, as this can take a long time and the chisel-point pen is not good for shading.

SCOTT ROBERTSON:

THE LANDING

Okay, I hope this piece was worth the time and effort I invested in it. I wanted to do one big piece that had a lot of different ship designs, a big interesting cityscape, and several foreground characters. You can find a lot of my ship designs in this piece from the chisel point pen sketches on pages 54 and 55. In a piece like this you can really get sucked into spending more time than you should for a print that is this size. The painting started with the marker sketch above. You can see I retained a lot of the building design elements and the basic composition from this sketch. There are, of course, areas that I feel need more work but I ran out of time and energy to do anything more to it for this edition of *Concept Design*. It is ironic that, after all the time spent on painting ships into this cityscape, my favorite ship is the one to the far, far right just below center, through the doorway at the end of the walkway. Of course this was also the fastest ship to paint; I know there is a lesson in there somewhere! If you have seen my work in *Concept Design 1*, then you know I have a thing for reflections. It is a holdover from the old Art Center car-design days. The next spread will show a few zoomed-in detail shots of this piece.

THE LANDING DETAILS

SCOTT ROBERTSON:

Detail 1, far left: You can see I tried to get this ship to look like chrome by reflecting the surrounding environment and its own tail fins, as would be the case if this were a real place. I purposely added a little extra atmosphere to get this ship, and the others in the foreground, to separate from the background and give the viewer a very strong sense of depth and scale.

Detail 2, middle: Here is one of the foreground characters checking his watch. Why? I'm not sure, so I'll let you make up the reason. The pools of water in the foreground are there for me to be able to do another couple of fun reflections. I could come up with any number of justifiable sci-fi reasons for their presence, but I believe honesty to be the best policy. Off in the distance is a building with a lot of activity at about the same elevation as this foreground landing. The idea was that this scene in the foreground would be relatively the same throughout this active future city full of busy flying ships. If you look closely enough, you will see

that even in the future it looks like at least one mechanic hasn't figured out how to keep his pants up. I'm not sure I would want this guy working on my ship.

Detail 3, above: I think this one contains my favorite parts of this piece. There is nice depth and a variety of materials, subjects, and surfaces. I'm also pretty satisfied with the ship designs seen here. I'm hoping to find the time to do a big print of this one for the studio. I have to admit, though, that I might want to spend a couple of more design and rendering days on it before I commit to that.

SCOTT ROBERTSON: # PURPLE BRAIN, LEAF CITY, REPAIRS, LAB

The piece above was inspired by the sci-fi images of the '60s. Again it started as a collage of photos I had taken of plants. With a couple of hours of painting, it evolved into what you see here. I imagine the room or place as something on a tall organic tower above an older '70s-style city. You can see the hint of blocky building facades through the tower's holes. I have really grown to love doing these fast color sketches since they have the potential to become finished pieces in the future or can simply act as story starters for a future series of sketches or paintings.

The three pieces to the right were all similar in process to the one above. They all started as a collage where I zoomed in using Photoshop to find interesting compositions that I would spend an afternoon painting back into. Christian Scheurer refers to this process as "combinatory play" in his DVDs on concept painting, and I find it to be a very refreshing exercise. The top and bottom pieces were found in a loose collage of shapes I made in Painter, which

I then layered and mixed together in Photoshop. The middle piece started in the same manner as the one above with some photos I had taken at a museum of very mechanical subject matter.

I imagine that the story of the top piece on the right is about a couple of friends getting together after work in an open-air, smoggy bar, and complaining about the bad air and how working way up here above the city is for the birds. The middle one is a spaceport on some far-off world where we see a ship in for repairs, while a couple of mechanics drift by on their diagnostic device. The last piece is an open-air lab environment where a couple of technicians are trying to assess the problem with the craft.

SCOTT ROBERTSON:

TECH ISLAND, CITY CRAWLER

Above you can see some details from the piece to the right. This one was done early in this book's development. At the time I had imagined the team in the lower-right corner to be on an expedition of discovery to a partially deserted city in the mountains. The need for weapons is not because of any danger they may encounter; instead, the weapons are there because they fear the unknown. The piece on the lower part of that page is a fairly fast color sketch I liked enough to include here. To be honest, I'm not exactly sure what is going on between the robot being driven up the building and the guy standing at the end of the walkway. It looks like they might be upset with each other, yet the guy in white might just be helping to guide the guy in the crawler to make his way to the top.

SKETCH, COMPOSITE, AND PAINT

These pages include the work from the Creating Unique Environments educational DVD completed this year. The process starts with a bunch of loose warm grey marker sketches done on vellum and Mylar. The forms are very abstract at this point and only hint at basic architectural and landscape forms. I try to get a nice range of value, so my brain interprets the sketches as having depth based on atmospheric perspective. Occasionally I add a horizon line, but it is not necessary to do so. The next step is to scan the marker sketches, throw them all on top of each other on separate layers in Photoshop, and start to composite them, which is when they look something like what is on the bottom of the opposite page. When I have one of these large pieces, I zoom in and capture a couple dozen potential environment paintings to look at later. After all of my new files have been captured, they're opened all at once and reviewed side by side. Generally, I like to spend 20 to 90 minutes working back into the piece to simplify the forms, refine the surfaces, and delineate any objects that were imagined when I first saw the piece. Think of it as a grown-up digital version of being a kid again, seeing things take shape in the clouds.

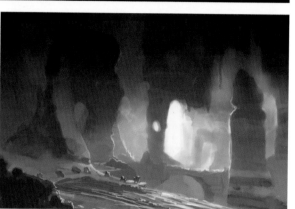

RANDOM STARTS

Here you will find a selection of raw, abstract marker sketches that have again been composited in Photoshop but not yet painted over. There is one in the upper-right corner of this page and some in the lower left and middle right-side of the opposite page. What I really like about doing these is that technically I hand-drew everything, but I do not think I could have if I had set out to do them in color, as they are now. The magic of Photoshop and digital experimentation, plus the many ways things can be composited and mixed, is a lot of fun. The other pieces are all starts to pieces that may be visited again in the future. Sometimes they start as story ideas, but usually I let the color and mood of the piece drive the story, and then I add figures to indicate the scale and support the story. As humans we have a predisposed tendency to search an image for other humans before we look for anything else. Knowing this, I like to include figures in my work to lead the viewer's eye to specific areas of interest.

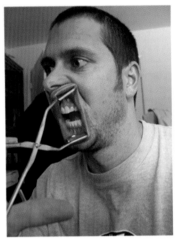

JAMES CLYNE:

SELF-PORTRAIT

I must admit, a bit of a departure from the rest of the book's content, but I thought I'd throw a wrench into the works by mixing up the predictable conceptual art with something a bit more representational of my dark side. I'm defining this as a conceptual digital make up test; I've created something digitally for the purpose of real-life practical make up application. For the past year, I've been collaborating with my writing partner, David Farley, on a feature-length screenplay from one of my horror short stories. This adaptation centers on an outbreak that leads to this ghastly makeover. Instead of creating a test on a real person, I have chosen to take a stab at it first in Photoshop.

I started by taking several digital headshots of myself. Some were the serious-actor type. Others were less austere and had the intent of exposing my teeth and gums. I accomplished this task by prying open my mouth with a kitchen tool in one hand and snapping away with the other. I experimented with several gourmet gadgets before settling on the tongs. The desired effect? A face only the mother of a baboon could love. I then comped the two together and, with the aid of Photoshopped raw meat, painted in the newly torn flesh and decaying skin. Violà, the transformation was made without ever actually applying nasty, caked-on make up to my face.

"PIETA"

JAMES CLYNE:

A SLIVER OF HOPE

I am fascinated with feature-film costume design because in a single frame the character's history and environment can be revealed. My inspiration often comes from pre-existing cultures. The gentleman's wardrobe, for example, was influenced by Middle Eastern attire—shawls, robes, and tunics. The subtle details in costume design not only add layers to a character but also truly reflect the personal distinctiveness felt by each member in the audience. That connection allows a story to feel organic even with its own peculiar boundaries. I find the best work is visually stunning, and more importantly, conveys a solid narrative. It's up to the viewers to complete the story in their own personal interpretation.

I first started the piece by loosely sketching thumbnails in a small sketchbook I try to carry with me wherever I go. I think this is important for any artist. You never know when an idea may percolate. After choosing a favorite composition, I then scanned the sketch into the computer where I used Photoshop with custom brushes to complete it.

j.Clyne

JAMES CLYNE:

HARWA MARKETPLACE

A recurring theme or motif in my work is applying cultural influences to new and unusual technologies and environments. This is an example of building a foundation of very real and understood structures and form language, and integrating these ideas into a new and exotic location. In taking this approach, I allow the viewer to first become accustomed to the surrounding spaces in the foreground, eventually leading them out to a world they may have never seen. I also try to give a human scale to the composition, allowing pedestrians to move freely throughout the piece.

The idea behind this work is a vast network of intertwining catwalks and bridges, clutching onto the sheer cliff sides of large, undulating rock formations. These formations rise above water level, their complex forms allowing townspeople to build light structures from natural materials such as bamboo and rosewood. This piece took quite some time to arrive at its final layout; many changes where made along the way in the computer. For example, the form language of the cliff side, and of the surrounding architecture, went through many iterations such as punching holes through the rock formation and adding more Asian influences to the architectural details. A small thumbnail was scanned into the computer and rendered entirely in Photoshop.

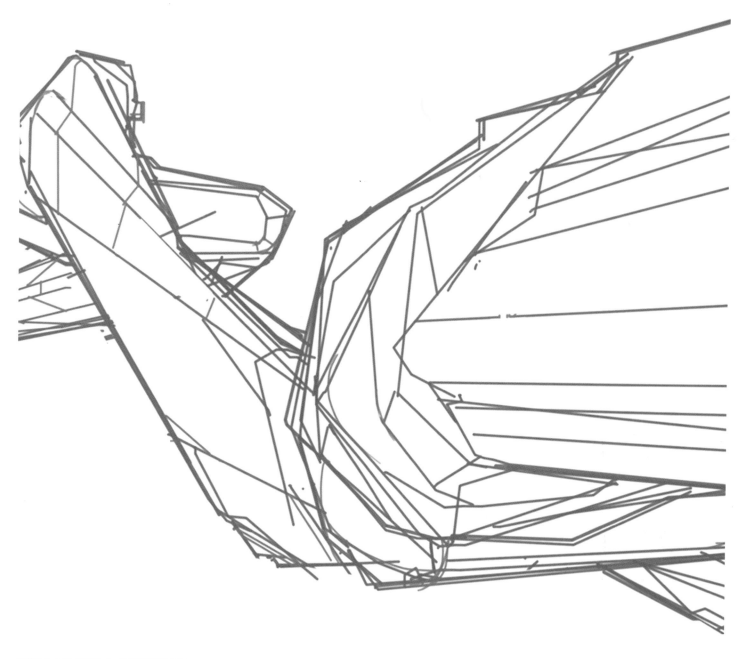

QUANTUM FETISH

JAMES CLYNE:

One thing I try to do in my work is find correlations in art and science. As an artist with a severely starved left brain, I'm fascinated by, and don't entirely understand, the language of such subjects as math and physics, although I'm always attempting to achieve a small understanding through my art. Quantum mechanics and general relativity and their possible connection, the Theory of Everything or string theory, are subjects I find intriguing and very creative in nature. Through visual storytelling, this piece attempts to provide my interpretations of such subjects. One ridiculous story thought was that this was a miscalculated attempt at creating the physical manifestation of a wormhole. I know—what a bunch of malarkey. But the point I'm making is that these ideas, as outlandish as they seem, provide an open channel for the flow of creative juices. Furthermore, as a designer, I need to find a problem to solve. I need to create an equation, then find the solution to the equation through discovery and problem solving throughout the rendering and design process. Without it, I'm left staring at an empty page. This was conceived and rendered in Photoshop 7.0.

A JOURNEY WITH HIS DONKEY

This is another example of creating visual narratives in my work. Not only have I set up a narrative-rich environment, including elements such as water and mist, but I have also inhabited that environment with characters at some sort of standoff. However, I've purposely left out enough information to allow viewers to create their own conclusions.

Using several different photographic textures, I wanted to convey a sense of danger through various textural motifs such as on the sheer cliff wall encroaching in on the composition and the rough-hewn stone walls of the temple. Photoshop excels at fusing photographic elements with hand-drawn compositions. I'm always consciously reminding myself that the drawing dictates the direction of the composition, not the textural reference.

The image on the left was done earlier as a quick study in gouache on illustration board measuring only 2 x 3 inches. Working at this small scale allows me to see the whole image at a glance, rather than having to scan my eyes back and forth over a large full-page image.

THE TRASH BIN

JAMES CLYNE:

Rather than displaying an entire series of finished pieces, I wanted to show several works that didn't quite gel. One neglected aspect in the design process is the attention given to all the failed attempts at a finished piece. I have several incomplete examples here ranging from rough sketch to almost completed colored composition. In doing so, I wanted to illustrate the fact that not all of the designer's conceptions end in a healthy birth. Sometimes the composition, lighting, color palette, or subject matter just doesn't work out. I always try to be willing to discard and start over at any moment along the way, remaining creatively malleable up to the very end. Otherwise you'll find yourself spending hours on a piece you know just doesn't feel right. However, I still go back and look at these failed attempts, and may even return to them with a fresh look. The above page was rendered in pen and pencil on everything from a small Post-it to 11 x 17 inch vellum. The colored renderings were executed in Photoshop.

VENUS NOIR

JAMES CLYNE:

I collect original pulp and paperback cover paintings from the early 1950s to late 1960s. Favorite masters of the brush such as Robert McGinnis or Robert McQuire were able to bridge the gap between commercial art and the fine-art world. Typically painted on illustration board measuring only 9 x 12 inches (for timesaving purposes), these guys pumped out paintings on a weekly basis for the covers of pulp fiction movies with stories of murder, lust, and substance abuse. This was my attempt at folding in that vintage noir style with a touch of my own hyper future aesthetic.

Like old pulp masters, I intentionally composed the frame for the hypothetical insertion of title, author, and publication either above or to the right of frame. The piece is also intended to be more graphically abstract rather than a true representation of a dimensional space. I also wanted to achieve a sense of timelessness, meaning without specific genre of science fiction or film noir. This was rendered completely in Photoshop with the use of custom brushes for a more painterly tooth.

CYPRESS CITY

JAMES CLYNE:

This piece was part of a series of instructional DVDs I completed for the Gnomon Workshop and Design Studio Press entitled Rendering a Cinematic Environment. In the step-by-step process of rendering this layout, I covered such topics as dramatic lighting, mood, creating depth, and design theory. It was a challenge to accurately show what can be constructed within a short amount of time—overall I think the painting took only two hours—and still give enough information, detail, and insight into what it takes to pull off such a piece. I also went into some of the more advanced Photoshop procedures such as layer properties, brush techniques, and texture applications.

Ironically, I found the exercise to benefit my own thinking process while speaking about the piece as I was drawing. Sometimes I find myself getting a little rusty, so it's important to keep pounding the basics into your head over and over again. I started with an 11 x 17 inch line drawing on vellum, scanned it into the computer, and rendered it completely in Photoshop.

JAMES CLYNE:

CHUPACABRA

About a year or so ago I was approached by a director to conceptualize and develop a look for a creature in his low-budget horror movie. He was kind enough to allow me to present a variety of the initial sketches here. The creature is the fabled chupacabra, notable as a South American folk tale in which the creature sucked the blood of its prey. In discussions with the director, several design criteria arose including size, proportion, anatomical references to other animals, and design specifics for the head (the way the jaw articulated, head proportion to body, and hair density.)

Because of the tight production costs, I concentrated on keeping anatomical similarities with such animals as grizzly bears, hyenas, and especially the baboon. From there I focused on studying the facial gestures of such animals, expressions such as fear and anger. To further the intimidation factor, I chose to expose the teeth and gum line by opening the mouth area, connecting the upper and lower jaw with powerful bands of musculature. Sketches were done with Prismacolor pencil and ultra-fine-point ink pen. Several sketches were then scanned into the computer and manipulated in Photoshop by changing hair density and jaw location.

JAMES CLYNE: ## LOS ANGELES: PARTLY CLOUDY, CHANCE OF RAIN

This rendering started out from a digital photograph taken above Griffith Observatory in Los Angeles, California, in 2005. As I was hiking above the L.A. basin, I looked back at the endless miles of converging boulevards and lattice work of urban sprawl, and wondered how the view would change if a megalomaniac building developer came in and plopped a multi-mile-long structure right through midtown, snaking its way to downtown, and finally stretching its arms out to the coastline. Provided as mostly a sculptural design, I also wondered why trends in urban planning haven't taken a more horizontal approach to building development. Allowing these megastructures only to touch down on certain predefined areas, the footprints would be minimized for space availability.

Using the photograph I took as an under layer for the composition, I then loosely brushed in forms both positive and negative to define the layout in Photoshop. Once the overall form was determined, I spent the remainder of the time folding in the new Photoshop elements with the preexisting photo, always making sure the lighting and color palette matched. I learned this process primarily from studying the works of the old feature-film matte painters who used to paint on large panes of glass.

STEVE BURG:

VISITORS

These images reflect my ongoing fascination with the idea of "alien archeology." The main inspiration for the environment is Angkor Wat in Cambodia, one of the most striking temples of the ancient world.

A human archeological team has discovered this enigmatic structure on some distant planet. They have set up a small encampment at the base of one of the massive towers. One of the explorers is startled by the arrival of the visitors, which are clearly not human beings.

The main image here is a fairly simple environment created in 3-D. I experimented with different color and lighting before settling on the blue-violet color palette. Some of the alternate color schemes can be seen in the supporting images shown. This is primarily a straight 3-D render, although elements such as the tents of the human encampment were painted in Photoshop.

It's always troubled me that intelligent alien life is usually depicted as naked. After all, we wear clothing, so why would aliens be any different? I decided to depict these particular aliens wearing space suits, suggesting that while the environment of this planet seems to be suitable for human explorers it could well be inhospitable to their alien counterparts. These alien visitors are somewhat enigmatic; it isn't clear whether they are friend or foe.

From an illustration standpoint, I wanted to raise questions about the place and the aliens, and leave the answers entirely up to the viewer.

The other views may or may not relate to one another. They are the result of visual experimentation. The cavelike environment began as a very simple 3-D object from which I derived the basic texture and lighting. The final image developed in Photoshop, and I used the "liquify" filter to distort the contours. All the elements were blended together with subtle painting techniques. The last step was to introduce a figure to ground what was basically a completely abstract image and give it a sense of place.

STEVE BURG:

CITADEL

Left to my own devices, I do a great deal of visual experimentation, and the results often tend to be more abstract than work created to fulfill a client brief.

This exploration is largely unstructured. The starting point can be a 3-D image, a sketch that is scanned and painted, or a serendipitous "accident." I have a huge backlog of such images, and although they are not revealed to many people these experiments often inform my other work. There is not a lot of opportunity in most commercial art for unstructured exploration, but it is of tremendous importance to me and I expect to continue this ongoing exercise indefinitely.

Some of the images here seem to have an Art Deco feel. There is no story and no context other than what exists in the mind of the viewer. They appear to be architecture, but beyond that it is fairly mysterious. The loopy stone rings are a 3-D experiment, and I have no idea at all what they might represent.

The large image of the castle overlooking the ocean is more defined than the others, a good example of the move from abstraction to a more specific context. This image is more defined than most of my visual experiments, but it is not completely realized as a finished illustration. I could continue to add detail such as figures and other structures, but for better or worse I decided to leave the piece in its present state.

In the color and lighting, the intent was to capture a feeling of antiquity as opposed to futurism, although the large scale of such structures would dwarf any stone fortress from our own history. While I love futuristic science fiction design, hopefully some of these images evoke a sense of timelessness. Do they offer a glimpse into the future, or the distant past? All I know for sure is they are not the familiar world of today—and that's fine with me.

© BURG '05

© BURG '05

STEVE BURG:

CATACOMB I: SPHINX

I love stories of the imagination and invariably find myself thinking of possible scenarios while an image takes shape. In this instance, the story actually came first. The images here as well as the following two spreads grew from a concept for a short film. The various elements were created to bring this story to life in the form of 3-D animation.

The setting is a cold and inhospitable planet in another star system. A team of archaeologists investigates the relics of a vanished alien civilization. Sphinx-like statues stand guard over the entrance to a vast underground city. Soldiers have arrived at the site to evacuate the archaeological team.

The various elements were developed in 3-D, the result of numerous iterations on a theme. The sphinx underwent radical changes before arriving at the simple design shown here. Visualizing "alien art" proved to be quite challenging.

My personal take on all things alien is to omit as much specific detail as possible in order to evoke a sense of mys-

tery. Here the intent was to create a literal sculpture of an alien being, but the sphinx ultimately became much more graphic and stylized. I deliberately avoided swirling organic detail because in my view this has become a cliché. I'm not at all certain whether the end result is a successful representation of an alien artifact. Sometimes when the dust settles I look at the resulting piece and wish I could start over!

In contrast, the human space suits and land vehicles were much easier to create. It didn't seem necessary to reinvent the wheel, so I opted to play within well-established boundaries. The intent was to imply the harshness of this imagined off-world setting through a very rugged design. In addition to extremes of wind and cold, the atmosphere and soil of this world might be highly corrosive. The look of the human technology was influenced by deep-sea submersibles and diving suits. Any delicate components are heavily sealed against the hostile environment.

© BURG '05

STEVE BURG:

CATACOMB II: PROCESSING PLANT

There is more to this remote planet than mysterious alien ruins – it has a wealth of natural resources as well. In this view we find ourselves in the heart of a huge industrial complex created to process resources for eventual transport off-world.

This environment was influenced by the look and feel of present day mining and oil drilling sites. The extreme effort of extracting precious resources from the ground has led to an impressive technology. The machines that yield the life's blood of an industrial society must function in some of the most inhospitable conditions imaginable.

The vehicle featured here is a chassis that can be fitted with assorted modular components to perform a variety of tasks. In the context of my storyline it has been pressed into service as a personnel transport – which is not at all what it was designed for.

This vehicle started out as a series of line sketches that led to a 3-D mockup. Once the mockup was roughed out, I began working out clearances for the various articulations,

which often dictated the shape of a particular part. Once the basic configuration was worked out, each component of the vehicle was modeled in greater detail to give the final design the appropriate look.

I wanted to produce a futuristic vehicle that felt very functional, along the lines of present day earth moving machines. Each wheel is independently powered. The cab is entirely enclosed, and the vehicle provides power and life support for the driver as well as external hookups for passengers to replenish their suits. The cab has very large glass panes to allow for maximum visibility - so I imagine the defroster is running 24/7.

The air on this desolate planet might be breathable, at least for short periods of time. But then again – maybe not! Whichever the case may be, given the frigid cold and gale force wind it's just easier to wear a spacesuit, so that's what people stationed here tend to do.

STEVE BURG:

CATACOMB III: AIRLIFT

This is a view of the main landing field of the processing plant. A full-scale evacuation is in progress, orchestrated by the military. Faintly visible in the distance, huge refinery towers rise above the icy plateau. Mammoth ore transport ships taxi across the field, glowing crimson with the last light of day. Soldiers and ground crews struggle against a gathering storm as twilight descends.

This image brings together nearly all the elements originally crafted for a short film project. To date, only one shot has been completed, but at over a minute in length that in itself was quite an undertaking. The sequential images shown here are frames from the animation. The intent was to establish the overall environment, following the vehicle up a ramp and out onto the airfield into the activity of a large-scale airlift in full swing. I hope to continue working on this animated piece, although as always time presents a tremendous problem in completing personal projects of this scale.

When the time came to create an illustration, the monochromatic palette so well suited to the moving image did not work quite as well in a still format. I decided to introduce a complementary color into the key light, which solved the one problem but created another. It took considerable tweaking to retain the feeling of an icy cold world while introducing a warm key light. Whether the effort was successful is not really for me to say, but it was an interesting challenge.

Another challenge both in this image and the previous one was painting the falling snow. What made for an effective snowstorm in the animation was less than useless when creating the still images. In the end, the snow was painted by hand and blended into the image on half a dozen layers with numerous masks to integrate it into the scene.

ARCOLOGY I: ASCENDANT

STEVE BURG:

My intent with this series of images was to depict several stages in the life of an "arcology"—a self-contained city/habitat of the distant future. There would be little point in denying my long-standing fascination with colossal scale. Here we see the city at its zenith, home to tens of millions. Although I do not recall the exact measurements, this structure is contained in a single dome that is about forty miles across.

As is usually the case when I work on my own projects, there was no clear idea from the outset of where things would wind up. The process began with the modeling of some architectural forms in 3-D. A fair amount of experimentation went into painting the textures for the window areas, which were created in Photoshop. Ultimately, two sets of textures were created—one for daylight and one for night.

Lighting and texture are probably the most critical aspects of creating a 3-D image. The geometry here is not particularly complex, and the impression of scale is imparted mainly through careful lighting and composition. There is

ongoing debate about which 3-D application is really "the one." Each individual artist's needs differ greatly from those of a massive production pipeline. For the illustrator making use of 3-D as part of the image-making process, overall ease-of-use and the quality of the 3-D renderer are of primary importance.

Once all the various elements have been rendered out, they are composited in Photoshop, where quite a lot of 2-D painting is done to achieve the desired effect.

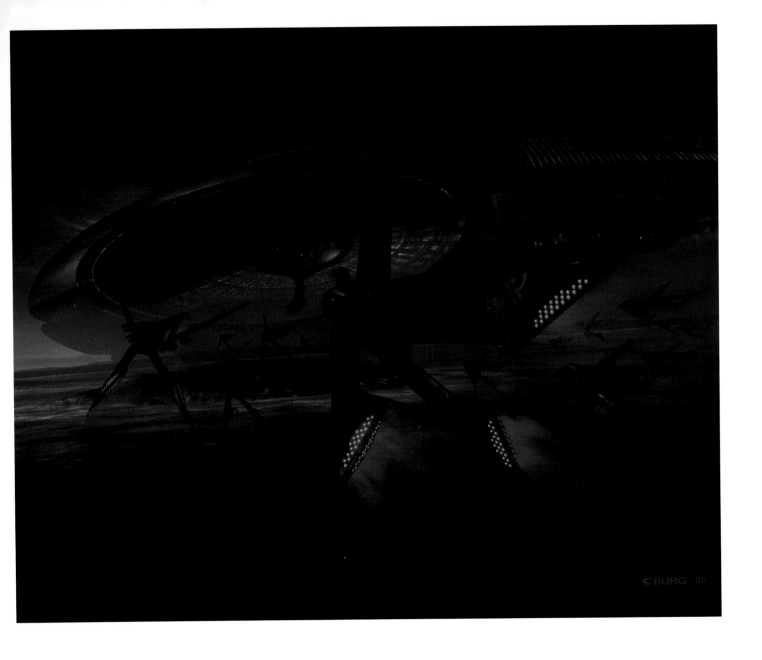

STEVE BURG:

ARCOLOGY II: THE FALL

What goes up must also come down. The arcology stood as a symbol of greatness, but it was not without enemies who lurked in the shadows, waiting for an opportunity to strike. Here, the city comes under devastating attack.

Heavily armed fighter-bombers streak in low over the coastline on final approach for their first attack. In the distance, the denizens of the arcology slumber peacefully, unaware of the threat that is fast approaching. As night wears on, the city is torn apart from within, its complex infrastructure reduced to glowing rubble.

In the first image we see the exterior of this preposterously immense city. The horizontal gap at the spheroid's equator is the vantage point of some of the illustrations in the previous spread, though individual towers are not evident at this distance. The elliptical entrance leads to a large aerial harbor, the point of entry for the attack.

The fighter craft were a lot of fun to create. They had to be readily identifiable as military aircraft, but I wanted the configuration to be somewhat unconventional. I usually begin the design process with a large number of quick line sketches. Rapid iteration is essential, and I strive for simplicity in the overall silhouette. I regret not being able to share some of these sketches here, but once they have served their intended purpose I often lose track of these drawings.

Once I have a sketch, I begin working in 3-D. Rapid iteration is equally important at this stage, as the design moves from crude block model toward greater refinement. My focus remains on the overall form until quite late in the process. The introduction of detail can prove distracting, so it is usually the last element to be addressed.

The second image made use of existing elements, with the introduction of interactive lighting for the explosions. The final image is the result of a lot of Photoshop painting, and the overall red palette emerged from a number of different color experiments.

© BURG '05

STEVE BURG:

ARCOLOGY III: MONUMENT

Here we see the arcology long after its fall. It is decades or perhaps centuries later. The city is abandoned, though the structure remains largely intact due to its sheer size.

Our modern cities are totally reliant on a high-technology infrastructure. Deprived of power, communication, and effective mass transit, they would quickly cease to be viable places to live. There are many historical precedents for the abandonment of cities due to changing circumstances, and I drew inspiration from research into the Mayan and Aztec ruins of Central and South America. My intent was to visualize a fallen Utopia, a city of the distant future in a state of ruin and decay.

The arcology's domed roof is so large it now contains its own weather system. There is frequent rain, leading to the formation of lakes and waterfalls on the city's inner ramparts. The central bowl has become a lake and is filling in with sediment and debris.

Initially I wanted to cover everything with advanced vegetation, in the same way that Mayan ruins are overgrown with plants. But it occurred to me that the materials breaking down in this future city might be highly toxic. Plants don't flourish on rotting metal and plastic, not to mention chemical and radioactive waste. In researching the ruins of the recent industrial age, I found little evidence of plant life, so the concept evolved to reflect a poisoned environment largely devoid of life.

I liked the fighter aircraft created for the previous spread, so I placed a few of them into one of the views here. Presumably made of advanced composite materials, these vehicles might remain intact for centuries. In any case, I wanted to include them.

To be honest, I am not yet entirely satisfied with these images. I will probably revisit this theme at some point in the future. It might be interesting to visualize this same locale a thousand years later. Perhaps by then the toxic waste will have dissipated allowing plants to spread, or maybe new life has evolved and flourished here.

© BURG '05

STEVE BURG:

BEHEMOTH

This series of images is something of a tribute to one of my favorite artists, John Berkey. An amazing and astonishingly versatile painter, he pioneered "epic scale space opera" illustration and – for my money – stands as the master of this genre.

The first image here was a deliberate attempt to craft a "Berkey-esque" spaceship in 3-D. I must admit that the project was never completed, but following a lot of 2-D painting the resulting image reached its present state.

The other images are some of the numerous stages of a project I worked on periodically for at least a year. The details of the scenario remain vague, although it is clearly a massive spaceship of some kind, attended by a fleet of smaller flea-shaped vessels. The background is a large complex without any apparent connection to the ground.

I always intended for this image to have a very smoggy atmosphere, and the palette was always amber fading down to mauve. So it remained, until one Saturday morning (very near the deadline, of course!) I woke up and decided to try a completely different approach. I relit the scene with a strong blue key light and a warm red fill, a scheme that's diametrically opposite what we usually perceive in the natural world. The final touch was to add the surface of a star in the lower right corner.

It can be challenging to create a sense of scale without familiar visual clues such as trees, houses, cars and figures, but it seems to be a challenge I often undertake. Fog can help to create scale and depth, and I rationalized that although these views are in space there might still be gas and dust allowing for a fog-like effect. In any event, the entire scenario is pure fantasy – you would never want to be that close to the surface of a real star!

I went through several iterations on the color scheme, which I did by mixing the channels in Photoshop. One of these is included here, although in the end I returned to my initial inspiration.

STEVE BURG:

SIGHTING

These images began as an exercise in exploring shapes in 3-D. For me this is a fairly frequent occurrence that meets with varying degrees of success—or failure, depending on how you look at it.

Sometimes an abstract shape will spark an idea. With the images here, the first pass resulted in a landscape of sorts. There is no telling what a shape will ultimately become—will it be a vehicle, a city, or maybe a shoe? Sometimes it's best to let the shape choose its own path.

In this instance, I felt my abstract sculptural form had potential as a gigantic airship. After some experimentation, I had the basic form: an odd cobra-head shape with a number of blimplike tanks and other details. I painted a texture in Photoshop, a large pattern of random stripes like those of a tropical fish.

Though not my intention initially, this colorful texture resulted in a look very akin to the classic spaceship art of Chris Foss. Although a version with a more typical surface treatment existed, in the end I decided to go with the yellow-and-blue striped pattern.

I composited the 3-D render into a digital photo of the sky that I had taken some months earlier. The sky was heavily repainted, with layers of cloud wreathing around the ship. The image seemed to lack something, so I put in a ground plane. For no particularly good reason, I incorporated another digital photo from the same batch as the sky—a barn. This seemed to belong in some strange way, so I painted a farm into the bottom of the image.

Is there logic to this? I am not aware of any. The entire process was entirely reactive and intuitive. In large part, that is the real value of doing pieces outside of the constraints of a client brief. To be able to explore, not knowing what you will find, is a great pleasure. More than that, I believe this kind of free-form exploration is essential for artists and designers to maintain their creative vitality.

© BURG '05

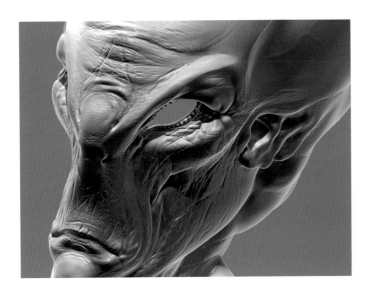

NEVILLE PAGE:

ALIEN HEAD

What can I say about the design of this piece? It's simply an alien portrait. What is interesting is how it was created. When I am creating a character on paper, my tools of choice are a Prismacolor pencil and Bienfang 360 paper. I like to explore and "sculpt" with the pencil. Sometimes my actions are deliberate, and sometimes they are exploratory and suggestive. I pause to see where the design is going and look for things that I had not preconceived. I call them happy accidents. For this exercise, I wanted to explore this process in a 3-D digital sculpting environment using software called ZBrush. This software was surprisingly very fluid and, for the most part, intuitive. Your ideas can be developed symmetrically, which is something clay does not offer. I am not proposing that ZBrush is a substitute for clay. It is simply another tool, and you have to know when to use it. This sculpt took five hours with design vacillations, however, and the colour version took another six (almost entirely design vacillations). There are pros and cons to either method.

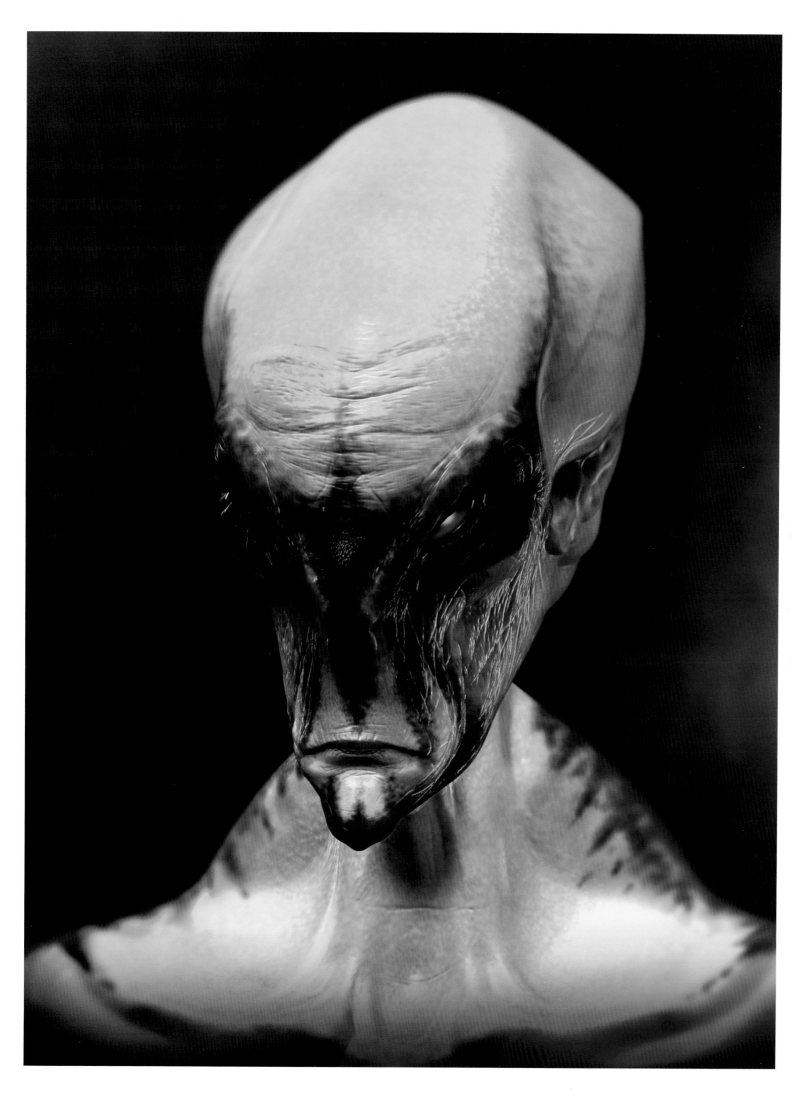

CAUDAL LURING

Some tree snakes have developed an incredibly inventive and deceptive way of getting a bite to eat called caudal luring. They perch on a branch, moving their tail in a way that resembles a worm. The movement usually warrants investigation by some unsuspecting morsel. Once close enough, the predation occurs. The animal on these pages employs the same technique, "worming" its tail on the forest floor. It would seem that this animal sits high on the food chain, but predators can also be prey. This is the reasoning behind the two sets of eyes. The front pair are predation eyes and the back ones are prey. These guys have eyes in the back of their head for good reason. Since they spend a great deal of their time focused on one spot while waiting for prey, the additional eyes keep them from becoming the same.

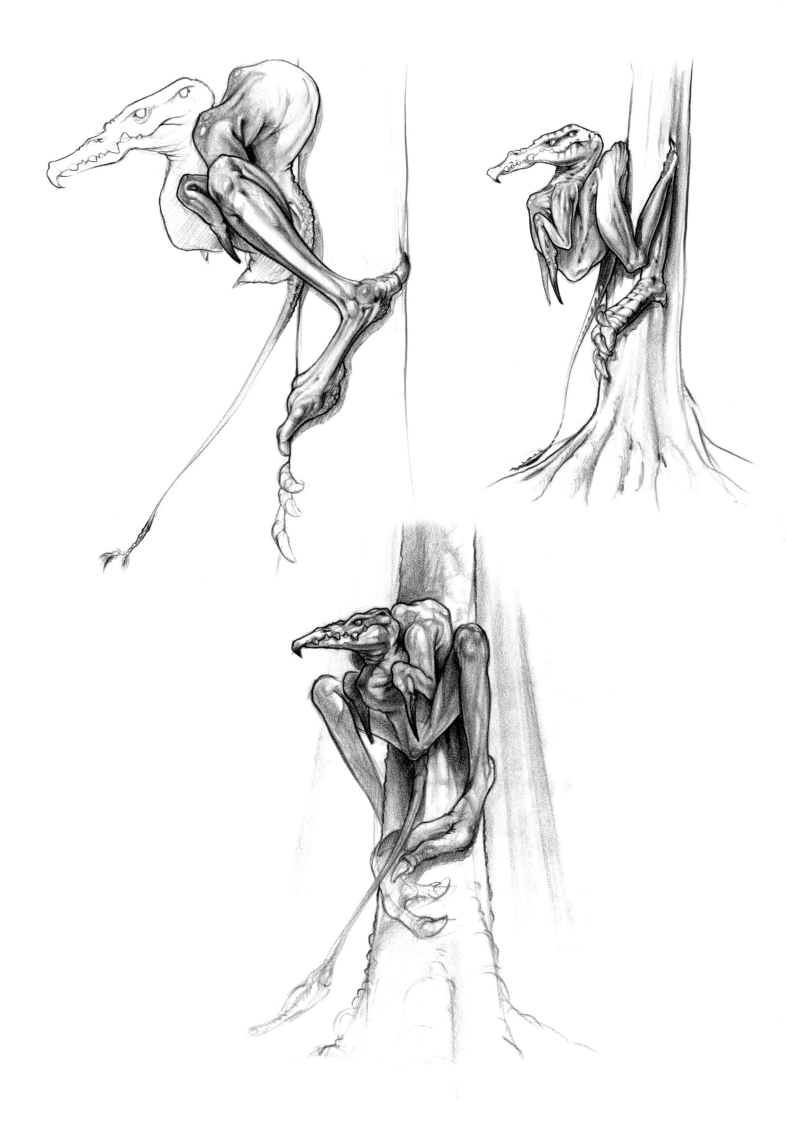

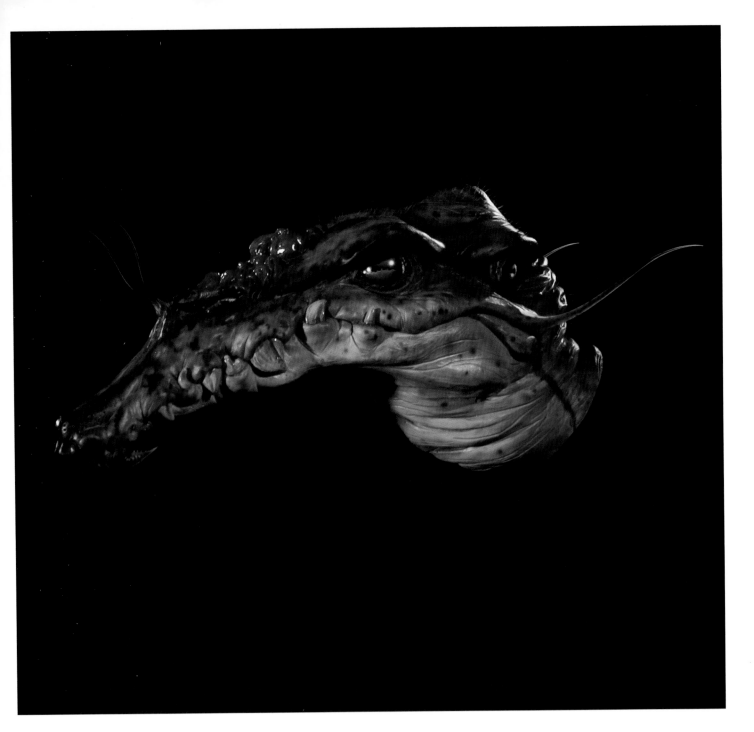

NEVILLE PAGE:

CAUDAL LURING 2

This design created itself. It began as a drawing warm-up assignment for myself. As it began to take shape, I defined its purpose. The sculpture was done only because I was itching to sculpt. In the end, the design lent itself to an immersive illustration. The original was done in Sculpy, molded and cast in urethane, and then painted by the fantastically talented Tim Gore. I later photographed it and did a Photoshop composite painting to give a sense of the creature in the environment.

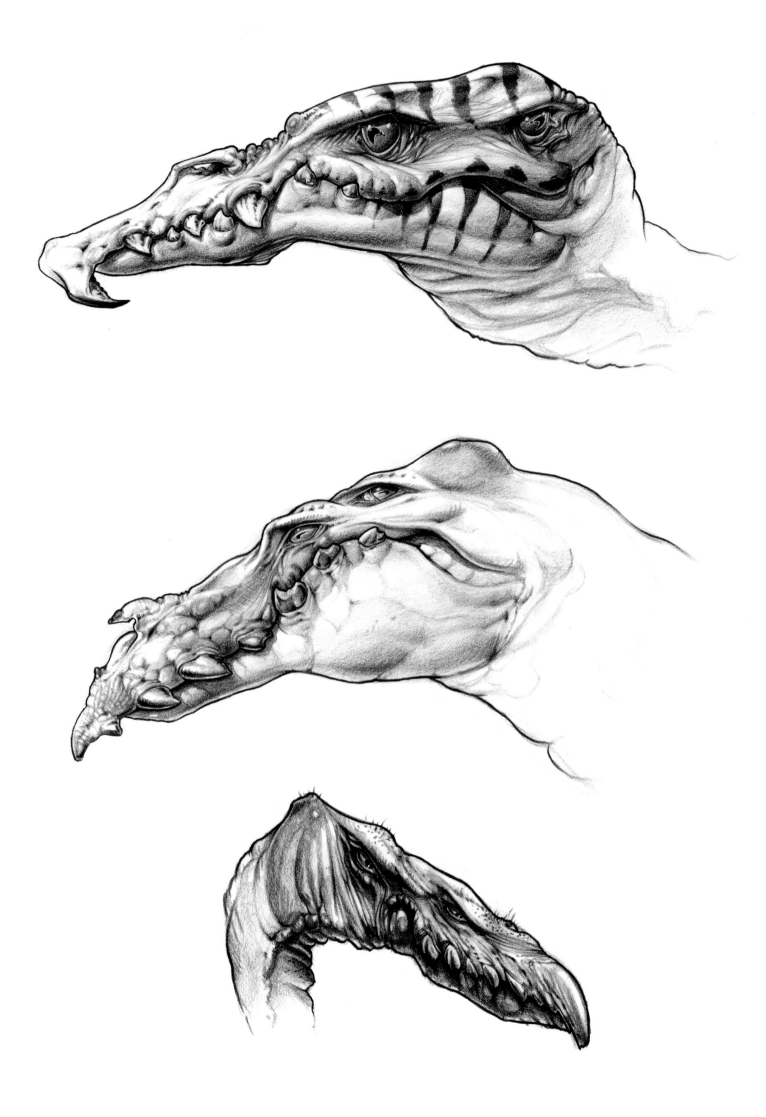

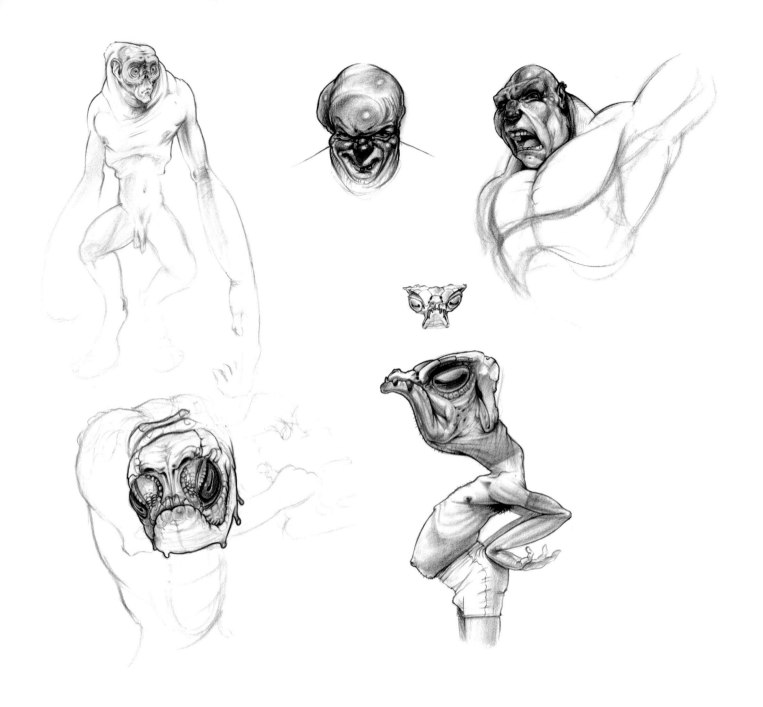

NEVILLE PAGE:

MISCELLANEOUS ANIMALS

All the drawings here were done with no project in mind and were purely exercise. Like an athlete trying to stay in shape, artists must exercise too. There is a paradox here, however, and that is the more fit I am as an artist, the less so I am physically. Could it be the hours I spend sitting at my drawing table?

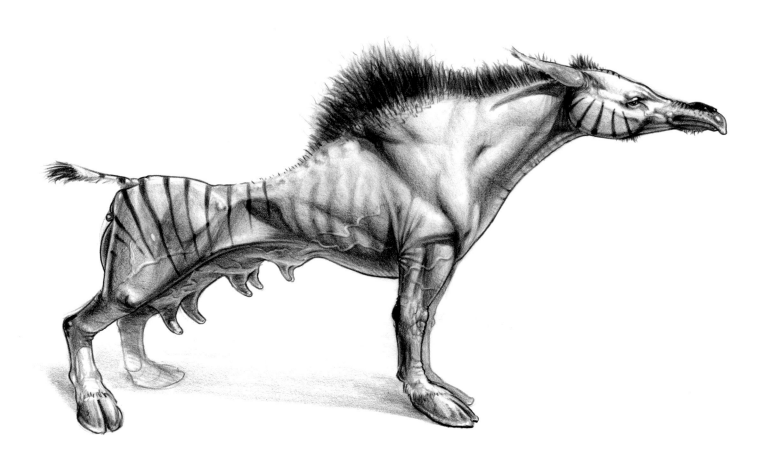

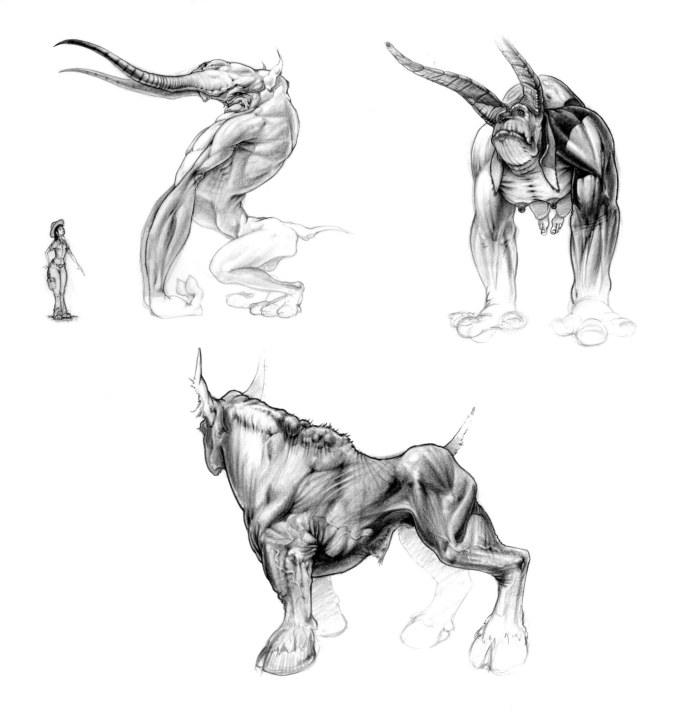

NEVILLE PAGE:

MISCELLANEOUS ANIMALS 2

To get really good at something, you must dedicate a large amount of time and energy to your practice. Think of the best athletes, musicians, and visual artists, and you will find that they are that way because they spend an obscene amount of time practicing. Sadly, I never seem to spend enough time staying artistically fit. Life often gets in the way.

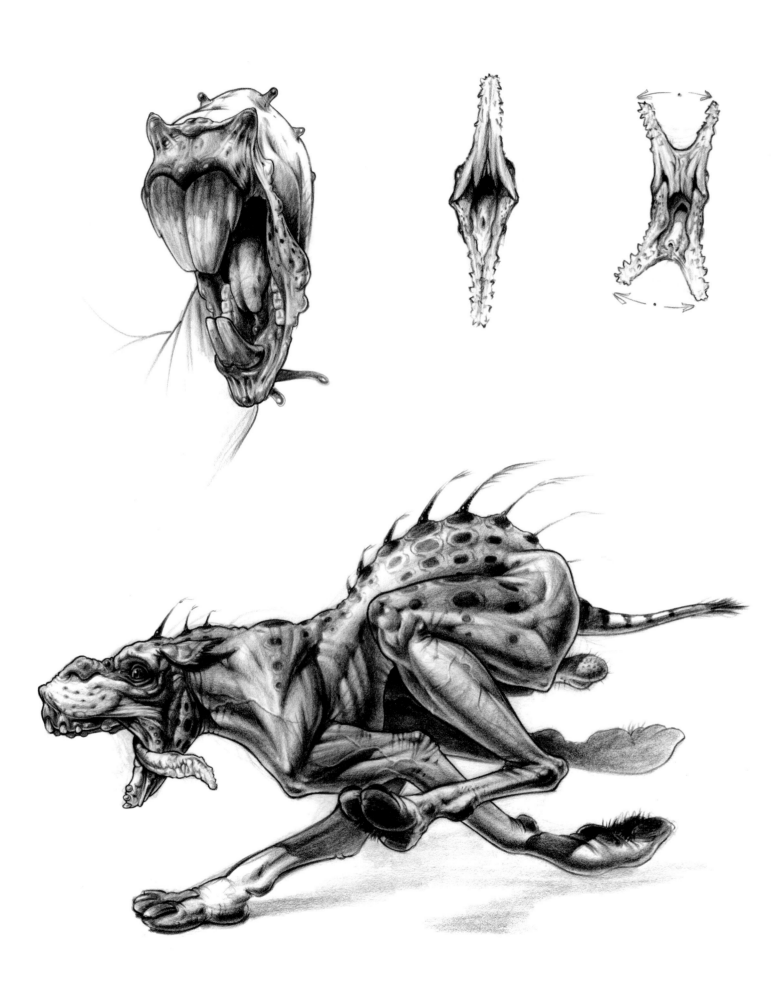

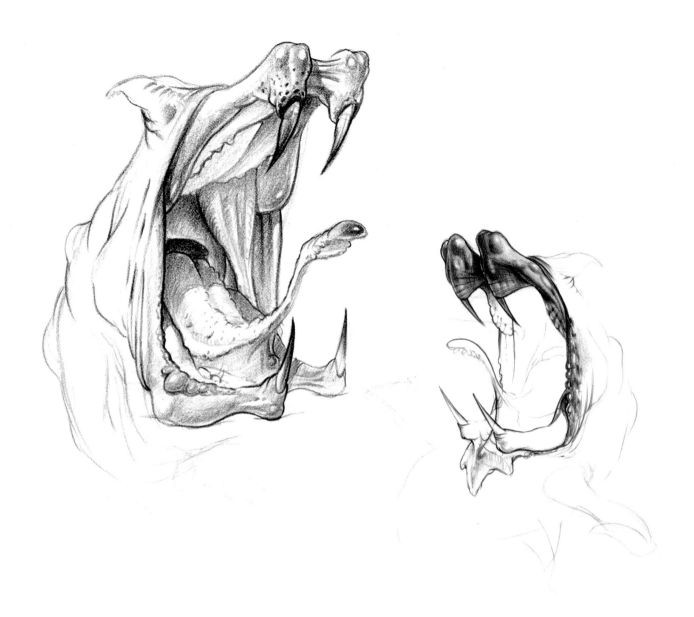

NEVILLE PAGE:

This critter was done purely for educational purposes. I wanted to do a DVD on rendering flesh using Photoshop. On a simple scanned sketch, I glazed away with pinks until the image was appropriately disturbing. Not a whole lot of time given to design, since it was all about the gaping maw. But my thought is that this creature is the size of a snail. I liked the idea of something really tiny having such a huge attitude. If you have had much opportunity to look at insects, everything about them is menacing.

MOUTHY

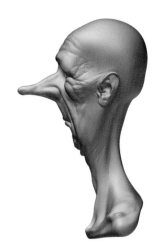

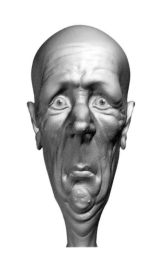

NEVILLE PAGE:

OLD MAN

I had my granddad in mind when doing this piece, although he looks nothing like this (his ears were a little big, however). The sculpt was done using ZBrush and then it was quickly composited and rendered in Photoshop.

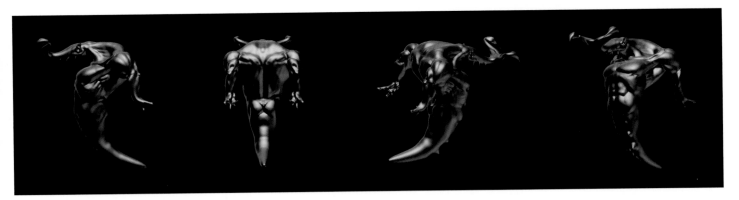

SNAIL MALE

A stream of consciousness approach to anatomy. For fun, I did the drawing on 11 x 17 Beinfeng 360 paper with Prismacolor and then blended the background with turpentine. It dissolves the waxy pencil and allows you to move it around with a brush or cotton pad. This was tricky to control, particularly around the perimeter of the character, but you can achieve great effects. I sat on this sketch for a while and then thought it was interesting enough to develop in 3-D. The goal was not to be exact but rather to use the design as a direction. Definitely an abstract piece and perhaps a little off-putting.

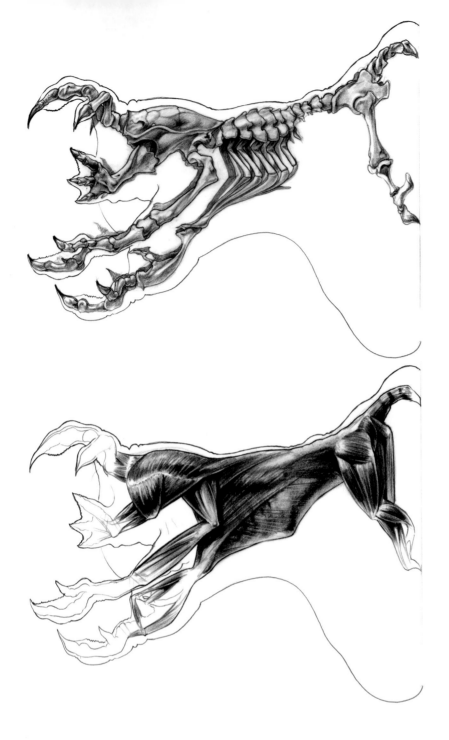

NEVILLE PAGE:

TREE HUGGER

Like a barnacle, this is an opportunistic animal. Upon find-ing a suitable spot, the creature seems to "bond" itself to the surface it was conceived upon and typically does not move from it. You could say the apple does not fall far from the tree when considering these completely arboreal ani-mals. Once they have set up shop, their entire lives seem to be spent in one spot waiting for opportunistic feedings. Offspring only migrate a short distance from parents, with their small footlike appendage. They also feed like barna-cles, opening up and waiting patiently for prey to come near. Of course, it helps that they give off a pungent, sweet smell to attract birds. Once they land on the inviting limbs, their consumption is lightning fast. With the exception of a few drifting feathers, there will be no remaining evidence.

This character was developed completely out of the desire to sculpt something in a clay known as WED. I thought I was going to do some sort of parasitic plantlike animal, and started scooping large masses of clay onto my

vague armature thinking that something would transpire. Even though I hadn't thought much about the character, I tried to impart as much physical reality as possible. Throughout the sculpting/developmental process, I was cog-nizant of its physiology. In fact, the drawings of its anatomy, although done after sculpting, were always in my head. I think that it is vital to understand everything you can about your character, whether preconceived or postprocessed.

NEVILLE PAGE:

WILDER BEAST

Frequently a design can be conceived of thoroughly in side view; vehicles, props, and characters are all subject to the sensitivities of proportion and one of the fastest ways to explore this is in a side-view sketch. This is mainly because you eliminate the time-consuming element of perspective. Also, if you are simply trying to establish the "character" (or attitude) of a design, focusing only on the silhouette is an even more efficient way to work. This is why I did a lot of black-marker side-view silhouette thumbnails to develop this character. Once the right "feel" was established (and this, of course, is a very subjective thing), the rest was easy. Like with most design, you start off with broad strokes and establish a strong foundation for the rest of the development. Meaning, once the silhouette is established, surfacing (adding the forms) follows. Then comes the graphic element and color. If the overall concept and form are bad, no amount of form development, detailing, and graphics will save it. It's kind of like putting on good cologne to mask a nasty smell.

HARALD BELKER:

Finalized in a Hot Wheels car for Mattel, this basic design has been with me forever. After I left Mercedes-Benz in Irvine, I had to design a new portfolio piece to get another job. The difficulty in working in a satellite car studio is that if your work isn't published, you've got nothing to show. The car industry is very secretive, and you just can't show things you did at work.

The details have changed significantly to fit into the Hot Wheels world. I thought a solid-chrome nose would be just terrific. The model came out great, and I love the fact that I had the chance to design toy cars and become part of that world for a while.

CORVETTE: LEVITATION STYLE

HARALD BELKER:

Corvettes from the '50s and '60s are still some of the better-looking cars in the world. Since the latest craze is to have cars hovering in movies, I thought, What would these older classics look like done up with a touch of Jetsons-style futurism and flying through the streets? Here are two images that show off the design's beauty with a twist of futurama.

I took pictures of these two Corvettes and even though the one on the left page is a bit more stylized, the one on the right is completely redrawn and rendered to give it that retro-future look.

HARALD BELKER:

By the way, this work does not reflect any of Porsche's views,
nor am I really trying to influence anyone at Porsche. They
are doing quite nicely without my help. With the 997 on the
market, I look at these sketches as more of an exercise in
details, nothing more. After all, it is really one of the more
difficult cars to design, yet they have become easier to drive.
I got two!

HARALD BELKER:

BUSTED

Happens to me all too often—police in the rear view mirror. The left side shows a quick study to the original painting, which turned into a loose sketch. This kind of line drawing is actually my favorite thing to do.

The front view on the right combines elements of the typical box-shape of 1970s cars with a high-tech grill that incorporates all kinds of gadgets. And I promise this will be the last time I use that background.

HARALD BELKER:

DVD TUTORIAL

This car is done in reflection of the DVD exercise, where I rendered a three-quarters front view of a car that I had sketched in the previous DVD. I had to do it one more time, which proves that your work will only get better with repetition. Taking my time and reworking a lot of the lines let me complete the car to my satisfaction.

Keeping it in the great tradition of automotive-renderings style, I showed a car that looks great as a sketch but is far from being realistic. The fun part of design and illustration? The overall image, the feeling—loose and tight at the same time.

SILVER METALLIC

HARALD BELKER:

Originally illustrated for a German magazine, I put this car in the book to show off the basic exercise of presenting a design to anyone. The side view holds the key to proportion, dynamics, and design. Everything else is working out details. Taking into account that wheels are bigger and side windows smaller, the illustration reflects the designer's ideal view of the car. Reality will be a bit different. The chick is eye candy again, just like those cheesy ads for car parts and tuner stuff. I kept her in silver as well, whatdaheck.

CHROME SLED

HARALD BELKER:

The chrome sled is a variation of the "Scraper." My intention was to find a good shape for rendering the car in chrome and to "future-ize" it a bit by adding some ridiculous details. The thing is slick and fast and looks fun.

The challenge was the chrome, i.e., finishing or rendering the metal without making it look like a bad, stereotypical, blue-sky-hard-reflection-to-yellow-ground-color thing. You can see, though, how something reflective really comes to life when parts and pieces actually "reflect" as a mirror image.

HARALD BELKER:

HB-X

This car just may be my claim to fame. After having only a week to design it for *Minority Report*, I reworked it so that Mattel could build a Hot Wheels model of it.

Out of the blue, another sci-fi flick picked it up. I can't mention the film, but it will be obvious when all of a sudden a futuristic vehicle shows up in a sort of tomorrow-world with today's cars.

The sketches on the right present the drawings for the toy. The rendering on the left page was done for my fourth DVD with the Gnomon Workshop and may be the last and final round of this design.

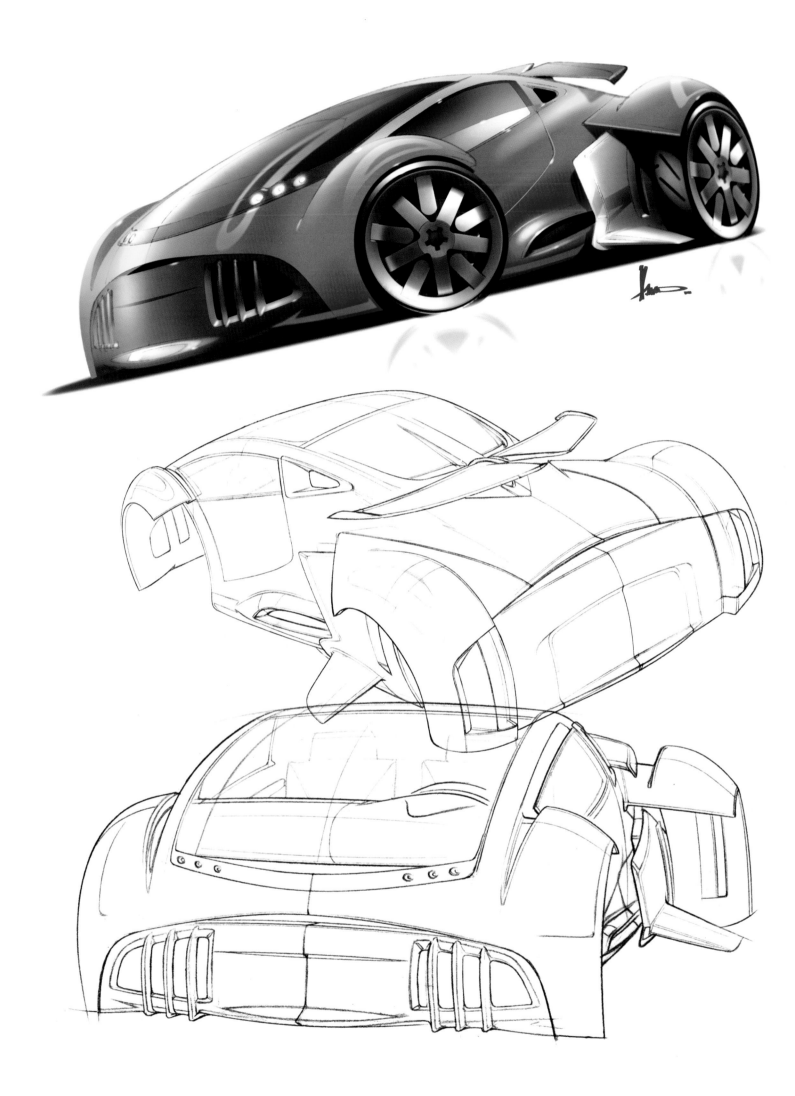

HARALD BELKER:

MACHINES

Robots and flying junkyard machines. An exercise in designing a dirty, old pseudo future-machine or a high-tech robot. I had intended to keep the robot fairly loose, but fell back into my comfortable tight style. I've got to loosen up. The background on the right is a combination of photograph and paint. The robot itself is a walker with major weapons as arms. The toe laser helps to keep it balanced.

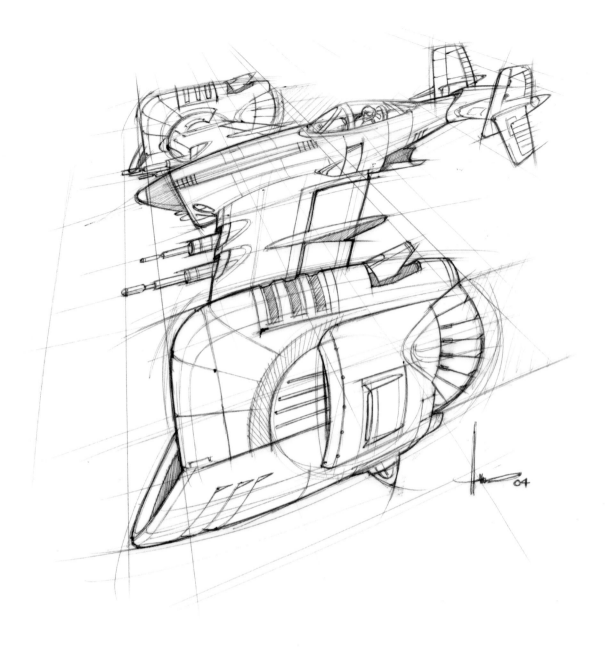

HARALD BELKER:

WAR PLANE

Over the summer of 2004, I was hired to develop a fantasy airplane for a game company. During the weeks of sketching out general directions, we never got to where the art director was comfortable with showing any of my work. Before too long, I was replaced by another artist. So, with the idea in my head of how I would have designed it, with some changes to differentiate the design from the actual project, I thought the book would be a good place to show a finished illustration of my take on it.

SPARTH (N. BOUVIER)
RYAN CHURCH
DYLAN COLE
KASRA FARAHANI
SEAN HARGREAVES
KHANG LE
ED NATIVIDAD
WARREN MANSER
STEPHAN MARTINIERE
RICK O'BRIEN
DAN QUARNSTROM
CHRISTIAN L. SCHEURER
OLIVER SCHOLL
FARZAD VARAHRAMYAN
MIKE YAMADA
FELIX YOON
FENG ZHU

In this portion of the book you will find work from 17 of our friends. For this volume of *Concept Design* we wanted to expand the book, and this section represents the crew we rounded up. I hope that *Concept Design 3*, if it should come to pass, will be even more diverse. We hope you enjoy their work as much as we have enjoyed their company.

SPARTH (NICOLAS BOUVIER):

CARAPACES

Above:
1. Sleepy Town
2. Sword Sanzer

Right:
2. (top) The Drag
3. (bottom left) Click Drones
4. (bottom right) Fast, Easy, Accurate

These images belong to a series of concepts done between December 2004 and February 2005. It shows, with an experimental approach, how organics and robotics may be blended together in order to create new forms and rhythms. They translate best the feeling of confused organization that often appears in my pieces. I especially like working on the combination of metal devices, wires, and disorganized pipes covered by large protection plates. It gives a very balanced aspect, even to larger structures. The connections between simple and more complex surfaces and areas add a realistic touch to the overall design.

The pleasure, when using digital painting tools, is that there is always a way to keep the designs and sketches live and nervous. The digital creative process is always in motion, always allowing new discoveries, especially when you leave the door open to abstraction.

Sleepy Town:
A very unusual spaceport located within a city.

Sword Sanzer:
The remains of a huge abandoned structure.

The Drag:
A sci-fi scene that includes a gigantic spaceship entity being dragged by smaller vessels.

Click Drones:
This piece was done in order to experiment with color themes on rusted metal surfaces. It remains a very abstract piece in many ways.

Fast Easy Accurate:
A new robot prototype standing in a futuristic battlefield.

RYAN CHURCH: # DRIVE-THRU, FISHING, BALLOON BEASTS

I painted these three images in my spare time while working on the last *Star Wars* movie. At my day job, the fun "blue sky" phase was winding down, and I was doing a lot of detailed art direction at ILM—these three pieces let me get back into the fun of doing some quick concept design. An added bonus was the chance to give myself an assignment; that's an opportunity a designer rarely gets.

Drive-Thru is a sci-fi take on an otherwise mundane subject matter; it's another in a series I've set in an upside-down city where buildings hang from superstructures like stalactites. There's also another idea for the proverbial "flyin' car," a recurring theme I'll keep trying out until somebody actually builds one that works.

With *Fishing*, I wanted to show an idea for an advanced off-road vehicle that rides around on tracks and can get up on its toes to walk over especially rough terrain by stretching out on articulating leg-suspensions.

In *Balloon Beasts* I wanted to depict a sense of move-ment and speed; in its earliest stages the subject matter was less important than the composition but as I worked through it, I wanted to show off a flying-car design and add a narrative element in the form of the attacking balloon-things. I don't know if the wheel-rotors would work, but they look kind of cool.

Once I settled on the content of each painting, I approached it as I do most of my digital artwork—a very loose and low-res initial value sketch to establish composition and design, then moving to detail addition and a few sidebar design explorations to figure things out. This project was a lot of fun—it was a great chance to work with a lot of talented designers and see what they could come up with when all the usual limitations were removed.

DYLAN COLE:

CITIES

Above:
1. (top) Urban Plateaus
2. (bottom left) Cave City Sketch
3. (bottom right) Night City Sketch 45

Right:
4. (top) Tropical City
5. (bottom) Lava City

For the top piece on this page, I wanted to explore the idea of a futuristic city where real estate is at a huge premium. I pictured structures built so closely together that they eventually become large masses shaped like buttes, maximizing the waterfront property. The two sketches above are color-and-compositional studies done in Photoshop. I really enjoy designing with paint and color as opposed to traditional media paint or markers. I just start with large masses of color and gradually refine the details and colors.

The top piece on the opposite page is a painting I created for one of my Design Studio Press–The Gnomon Workshop DVDs on matte painting, starting with a pencil sketch and going through to final painting. I enjoy juxtaposition in my work and had fun introducing science fiction elements to a tropical scene. Creating a shot in stark daylight is very difficult because of the light's unforgiving nature. It is much easier to have a lot of haze and atmosphere to hide details.

KASRA FARAHANI:

Above:
1. Striped Canyons of Noon

Right:
2. (top) Lumbering Bazaar
3. (bottom) Mid Noon

EXCERPTS FROM NOON

This series of images are from a project called Dark Side, which I developed with fellow designer Ari Bilow. The idea for this project came out of one of those broad-stroke philosophical conversations that coffeehouses tend to foster among friends.

In discussing the developed world's insatiable appetite for fossil fuels, we began to wonder what would ultimately wean humans off of fossil fuels, and what the resulting world would look like. We imagined that desperation for fuel would lead to persistent drilling at the poles, to deeper and deeper depths, as resources became depleted. At some point the geological integrity of Earth would be compromised, and violent seismic activity would follow: an earthquake that lasted 100 years. At the end of that time, there would be a hemorrhaging of liquid rock at the source of the most aggressive drilling, and this newly hardened tumor would be so substantial as to throw off Earth's center of gravity, causing its elegant spin to become catastrophically lopsided and erratic. This would result in a world without day-and-night cycles—a world with a fixed relationship to the sun. At one pole would be a barren region, Noon, where the sun blasted directly down 24 hours a day, and at the opposite pole would be a frozen land in constant darkness; the intervening lands would be a gradation between these two extremes. These images visualize a polarized world where vital resources are almost exclusively contained at opposite ends of the planet.

SEAN HARGREAVES:

MAS DECOSTIJL

Above:
1. (top left) Fleuro 7
2. (top right) Fleuro 9
3. (bottom) Ohm-4 / Romanov Ulitza

Right:
4. (top left) Omnon
5. (2nd from left) Pyrxx
6. (3rd from left) Off
7. (4th from left) Icarus
8. (bottom) Ohm-4 / Pereulok

These two pages hold images that were first sketched and then detailed in a line drawing that was scanned and rendered in the computer using Adobe Photoshop and Corel Painter. No 3-D software guides were used. The images are personal projects.

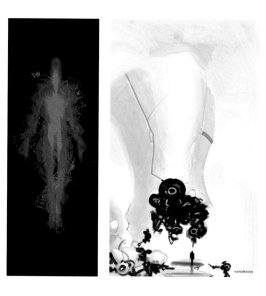

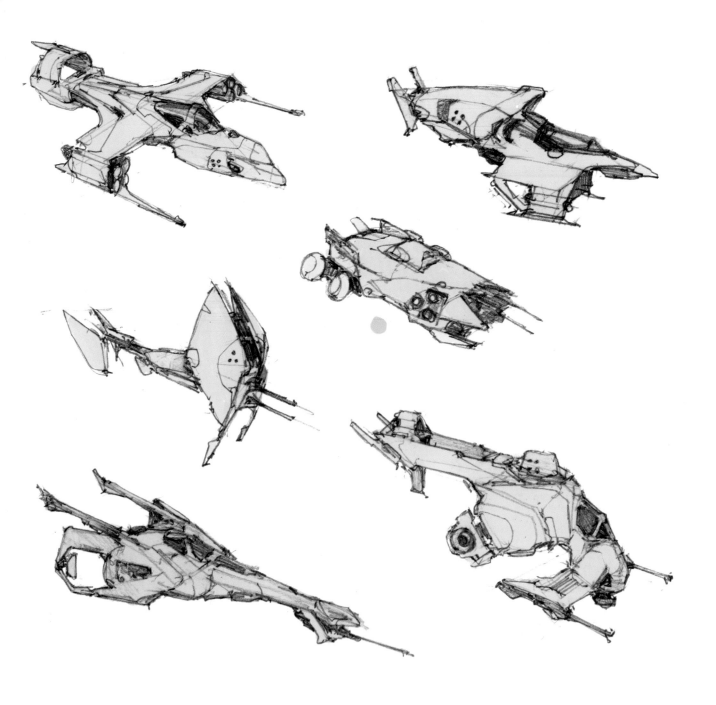

KHANG LE:

PARKING STRUCTURE

I like to start my designs with a set of thumbnails. It helps me explore a variety of shapes, instead of creating something I'm comfortable with. The thumbnails that I picked have an interesting triangular front-shape that intrigued me. I start out with a regular pencil and finish up in Photoshop. Once the drawing is scanned into Photoshop, the next step is fixing the perspective. This is necessary because I like to work directly on top of my original thumbnail instead of doing a larger drawing. An easy way to check my perspective problem is by mirroring the image. I can do this in Photoshop with the flip horizontal function. Once the perspective is corrected, the next step is glazing the basic tonal value of the painting. I saved the dark shapes in the foreground, keeping a high key-value on the city below. This helps push the elevation of the parking structure to a towering height.

ED NATIVIDAD
© 2·8·94
"THORACIC CAVITY"

SURFACE AREA IS MORE
PROMINENT IN LEGS AND
IS SLOWLY SUBDIVIDED
TOWARDS UPPER TORSO.

ANATOMICAL VEHICLES

ED NATIVIDAD:

These two images reflect my prevailing interest in conceptualizing armor, which decorates or disguises what it protects. They are part of a series of drawings that explore armor for man, animals, and vehicles.

There is an infinite range of styling outcomes using standard human dimensions as a starting point. Inventing the scenario of a human projectile is how the cannonball sketch began. Structural integrity during impact was a concern as was the welfare of the suit's operator. The sphere was used to protect the axial skeleton with the arms recessed within, leaving the legs free for mobility.

The antithesis to this design could be the above sketch, which is abundantly cosmetic rather than functional. The idea of building an iron fence around the subject was inspired by the architectural detail of buildings designed by Louis Sullivan. This aesthetic may be interesting, but is not practical for protection.

ED NATIVIDAD
LOW TECHNOLOGY ARMOR
VINTAGE MODEL PRE-
REVOLUTION ERA

WARREN MANSER:

EXCERPTS FROM CONSTELLATION ORION

Above:
1. The Goddess Ishtar

Right:
2. (top) Mount Mashu Summit
3. (bottom) Ishtar's Arrival

Ancient Sumerian tales spoke of a race of beings they called the Anunnaki, or Those of Heaven Who Are on Earth. The Anunnaki were lead by a pantheon of 12, six males and six females, with each member corresponding to a constellation and a member of the solar system, thus forming the bond between the celestial zodiac, Earth, and the heavens. This pantheon governed all the events on Earth and was responsible for the creation and civilization of man.

The Anunnaki were called Nefilim, or Those Who Were Cast Upon the Earth, and They Were the Mighty Ones of Eternity as well. Every ancient culture spoke of them, but with different tongues. Some would call this mountain Valhalla, while others claimed it as Mount Sinai. The Greeks would call it Olympus, and it was the home of the immortals. The Egyptians described it in stories about the pharaoh's journey to eternity. Regardless which culture interpreted the ancient legends, the Sumerians were the first to speak of them, and they met on Mount Mashu in the land of Sin, to decide the fate of men. Their sky chambers glistened in the rays of the sun, spewing fire and whirlwinds, as they scaled the mountain to deliver the 12 to the great temple.

Ishtar was the twelfth member of the pantheon, and long before the tower of Babel was destroyed, she was called Inanna, or Great Lady of An, the great leader of the Anunnaki. She was also called Asarte, Aphrodite, and Venus. A goddess is beautiful and enticing, but beware, mortal men–Ishtar has used her beauty to seduce and destroy before. Legend speaks of her traveling across the sky in a great winged disk encircled with eyes and gleaming like burnished bronze. Finally she has arrived and is being carried up the great pyramid on her litter. As she crosses the threshold guarded by two great lions, we must wonder why she has been called to this assembly of the gods?

Source: *Stairway to Heaven* by Zecharia Sitchin (1980)

STEPHAN MARTINIERE:

NAUTILUS

When I started this painting, I was unsure what the end result would be. The starting point was a book cover I did called *Building Harlequin's Moon* by Larry Niven and Brenda Cooper. The story is about a small human colony terraforming a moon in a distant future, using enormous automated machines. The vehicle I created was half train, half harvester. Although I was pleased with the result, I felt the desire to see something bigger in scale. After experimenting with different ideas for a floating vehicle, some very organic shapes reminiscent of seashells started to emerge. I thought it would be interesting to create an environment reminiscent of an aquatic setting.

How would an underwater species evolve out of its environment and still retain some of its original aquatic design, say a thousand years in the future? I always like to think of connections between all the elements in a painting. The challenging and exciting part is to design from existing forms in the underwater ecosystem, and extrapolate those forms into terrestrial and aerial environments. The organic connection in this painting is not structural but more visual. Biomorphic. I want-

ed the elements to remind me of specific organisms like the nautilus, the fan-shaped sponge, or the jellyfish. Fins could have evolved into some organic solar sails powering biomechanic ships. I particularly like the structures in the distance. They rise in an intricate assembly of very thin, white blades and curves reminiscent of fish skulls. They have a certain elegance and lightness that seem to defy gravity. I didn't sit for hours at my table like I sometimes do, exploring numerous shape and concept possibilities. Had I spent more time I could have come up with very different and possibly more interesting shapes, but this was not a commissioned assignment. The process for making this painting was more organic, more spontaneous. I was more interested in seeing it happen than I was in doing it. I was letting the colors and shapes dictate the next step; letting the end result be a surprise. The underwater species evolution idea was more of a guideline. I like this spontaneous approach as much as the rigorous process of concepts. They both have their intellectual and visual rewards.

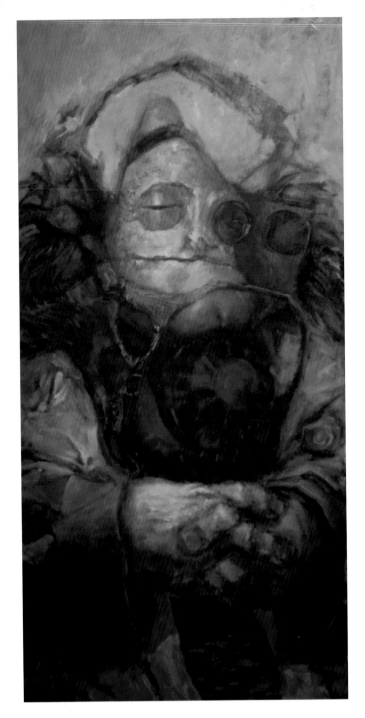

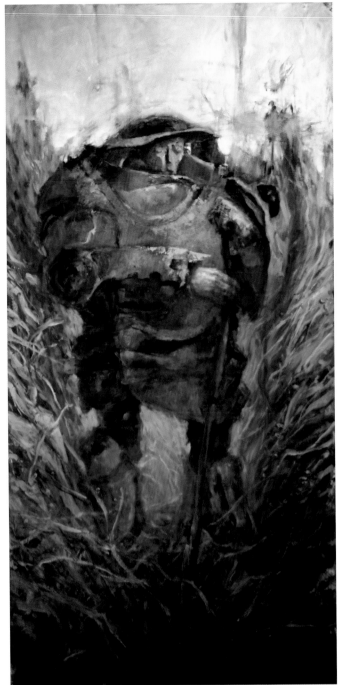

THE RANGE OF HUMANITY

Above:
1. (left) Judgment
2. (right) The Hunter

Right:
3. Blind

Blind, *Judgment,* and *The Hunter* are selections from a work in progress, which maps the human experience through metaphor.

The roots of this study date back several years to a period when my technical growth and creative vision vied for attention. Initially, the series took on a more traditional and literal structure. Characters reacted to situations and each other in a tangible environment. The story revolved around an inventor, his daughter, and a character known as Five. More or less the victim, Five was an ongoing experiment and vehicle for the father's ambitions, as well as a source of sympathy and compassion for the girl. As the work and vision matured, I began to feel increasingly tied down by the dynamics of the literal framework in which I'd enclosed myself. The common thread, however, had always remained the same. Five was the struggle and center of all things. He became the manifestation of human weakness and fortitude.

I feel fortunate to have endured such a long and challenging process. Creative growth and honesty of intent are difficult to achieve. *The Range of Humanity* has forced me to look ever deeper into myself by exploring the tapestry of human behavior.

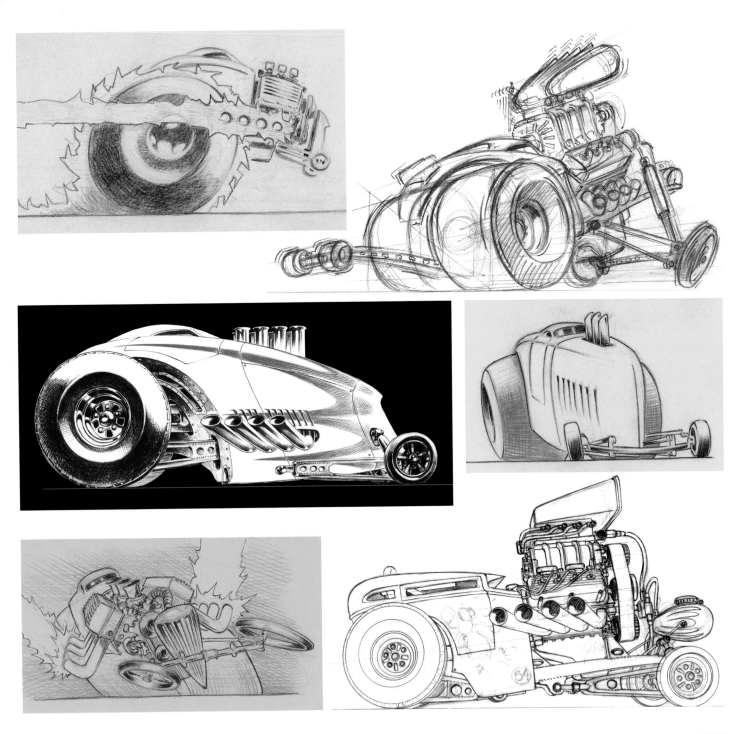

DAN QUARNSTROM:

JOYRIDE, FLATOUT

Applying Professional Standards to Adolescent Ideas:

The artwork on these two pages is the continuation of Joyride/Flatout, a lifelong fascination with hot rods, dragsters, and custom cars. I revisit this territory often, since it is the source of my earliest inspiration and has provided me with raw material to continue drawing. These are the drawings that I wanted to do when I was 12 years old. The pioneers of "wild style" car design, "Big Daddy" Roth, Dean Jeffries, Darryl Starbird, Gene Winfield, the Alexander Bros., and George Barris, provided a panorama of challenges for thousands of aspiring pencil jockeys and sustained my interest in the mechanical as "art." The principles I internalized then–about volume, weight, shape, construction, attitude, mechanics, precision, and patience–I now use professionally on a daily basis.

Most of the designs began as quick, fairly tight sketches on Post-its. My approach is decidedly "old school." I draw with Col-erase colored pencils and clean up the line with a Papermate Flexgrip ballpoint (fine) pen.

Post-its are my favorite medium for getting my ideas down quickly. Working small allows me to run through many variations of similar themes. The investment in time is minimal, usually 15 to 30 minutes. If an idea doesn't develop, I don't feel compelled to continue because I haven't invested too much time in it.

The Post-its become the farm team for further development. I keep them in a sketchbook that I consult when I'm looking for new ideas. The good ones rise to the top. I enlarge the Post-its on the Xerox machine to 8 x 14 inches. From the enlarged copy I make another very tight tracing using ellipse guides and French curves to keep everything clear and precise. The resulting drawing is tight enough to be enlarged once again to 16 x 24 inches. This enlargement becomes the basis for the final ink drawing. Using a light box, I transfer the drawing to two-ply Strathmore Cold Press paper. I ink the drawing using Rapidograph pens, once again using ellipse guides, ships curves, and French curves.

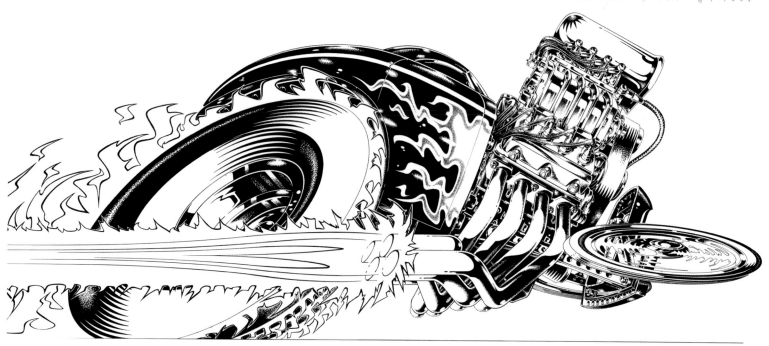

CHRISTIAN LORENZ SCHEURER:

PROCESSION OF EFFIGIES

Sometimes a change of scenery can have a dramatic effect on a designer's inner world and one can fall back into the childlike state of dreaming awake. That is what happened to me on a stay in New York, after having lived in Hawaii for several years. During the short trip, I filled a sketchbook with hundreds of architectural drawings and a number of sketches of characters, which inexplicably started growing organic wings, antlers, and appendages of plants and trees in a process I call "instant vegetablization." On the last page of the sketchbook, all the vegetablized people end up transforming New York into a strange tropical rainforest.

In regards to the painting, I thought it would be interesting to develop the transforming people as back-story for an imaginary carnival. In the painting, hundreds of spectators are excitedly watching a parade of effigies of ancient gods of transformation.

When designing fantasy, I believe it's important to rigorously establish rules and guidelines for the emerging fantastic universe. Like an anthropologist of the imaginary, I try to unveil the unknown world's secrets. Producing an elaborate painting like this one is a great way to create a world from the outside in. By loosely blocking in architecture and main shapes, questions of location, climate, and technology arise. When painting in the characters, more questions about societal structures such as race and social status have to be addressed. During the painting process, I try to answer each question one at a time. The more detailed the painting becomes, the more I find out about this new world and its story starts to unveil.

OLIVER SCHOLL:

SEEDS

Intent: Which two images could I create to present a reflection of my interests or abilities, which would introduce me to you, the viewer, and stand their own ground next to all the artwork in this book?

Layout: Given a one-page spread, I decided to have some fun with Scott's template. Rather than create separate images, I wanted to use two focus points taken from one image. The missing part may be filled in again by the viewer's mind, like the resulting image of separate film frames.

Subject: A classic space-opera theme. Colonization of an alien planet. A nanotechnological seed has been sent to grow the colony and colonists. Mankind is playing God, and its creation is giving birth to new life. I chose to use a classic subject but gave it a technological twist to be expressed through the use of nontechnological shapes and iconography. Often in my work, the ideas are inspired by stories. In this case, *The Diamond Age* by Neal Stephenson. Seeds is one of the images that was triggered by reading the novel. I

loved the depiction of a society based on nanotechnology and filled in this other side of it, although the scenario is not explicitly mentioned or part of the story line.

Execution: There were some initial pencil sketches and 3-D roughs in formZ, but overall, the image was created in Adobe Photoshop CS on a 17 inch Apple Powerbook with the use of a Wacom tablet.

Ad astra!
Los Angeles
February 14, 2005

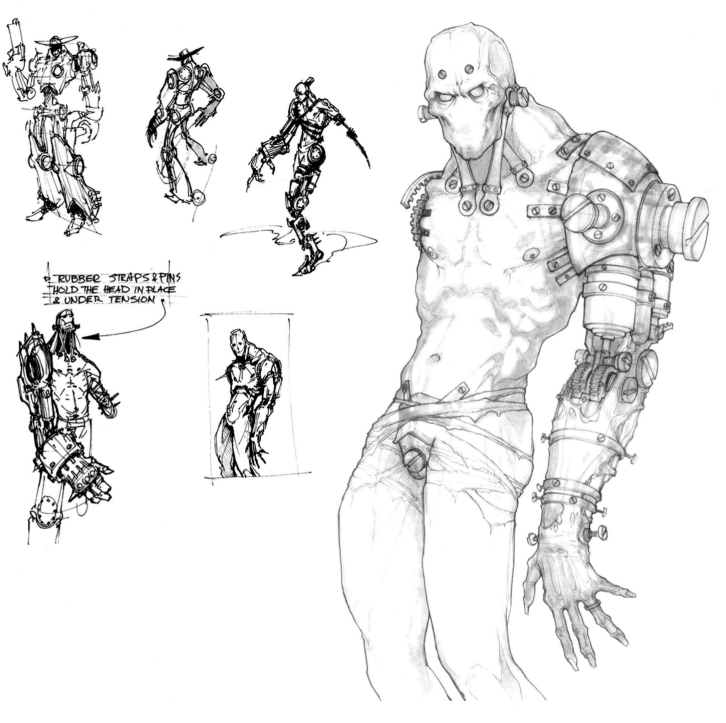

RUBBER STRAPS & PINS
HOLD THE HEAD IN PLACE
& UNDER TENSION

MECHBETH

FARZAD VARAHRAMYAN:

The background for this piece was my personal interest in combining organic and mechanical elements to create interesting characters. I personally think a character or creature who reveals a clue to their background is more interesting than one who doesn't. Take Darth Vader or Gollum. Grotesque creatures in appearance, but were they always this way? What corrupted them and turned them into the villains they are now?

Mechbeth, is a biomechanical junk heap, a tortured soul who could not be anything other than a monster. I hope the wedding band on his finger hints that at one point someone else loved him enough to marry him. So the question I'd like to raise in the viewer is, What happened to him, and what were the chain of events that initiated his transformation from loved husband into monster?

My basic rendering technique in Photoshop is very similar to using a dark Canson paper. I like to start out with a fairly thought-out design and line drawing, and then model the image by building up the highlights. I work in black and white initially and really focus on the design and form definition. Once finished, I will do simple image tinting to add a bit of color and additional mood.

MIKE YAMADA:

SKETCHES

I've always enjoyed working in graphite, and these two pages allowed me to indulge myself. I took a generic indication of a robed man for scale and went wild creating epic and slightly fantastic environments. I tried to make each unique and full of atmosphere; I wanted each to have the suggestion of culture and the remnants of some long-gone civilization. I found plenty of inspiration thumbing through old copies of National Geographic, and referred to elements that I connected with. For the actual drawing, I used a combination of powdered graphite, a pencil, and a kneaded eraser to pull out light areas and correct mistakes.

FELIX YOON:

REST STOP, FLIGHT

The first image is a parked vehicle under a rest stop. The vehicle itself isn't fully revealed, which leaves deciphering the image to the viewer.

The image to the right is simply a flying jet. The emphasis was placed on design, composition, and lighting on both pieces in order to keep the focus where I wanted.

FENG ZHU:

TEMPLE, CHARGE, NEW EMPIRE

For the past two years, I've been working solely in the digital medium—from the initial sketch to the final painting. It is a process I am still learning and will continue to expand upon. Working digitally has dramatically changed the way I approach my designs. Now I am able to play with colors, atmosphere, and textures more easily than with traditional mediums. These images are samples of this process. The top two images are tutorial paintings from my website. You can view their entire creative process at www.fengzhude-sign.com. The image on the right is a poster I created with The Gnomon Workshop.

HARALD BELKER

Harald graduated with honors from the transportation design program at Art Center College of Design in 1990. After graduating, he went to work for Porsche in Stuttgart, Germany, and then moved on to the Mercedes-Benz Advanced Design Studio in Orange County, California. His automotive design experience led to design work for the entertainment industry. Harald has designed vehicles and props for numerous motion pictures, including *Batman & Robin*, *Armageddon*, *Inspector Gadget*, *Spider-Man*, *Minority Report*, *XXX 2: State of the Union*, *The Cat in the Hat*, and *Stealth*.

Web site: www.HaraldBelker.com
E-mail: Design@HaraldBelker.com

STEVE BURG

Steve Burg was raised in New Jersey and studied film at the California Institute of the Arts. Burg began his career in visual effects and segued into design, working with artist Ron Cobb as a concept artist on George Cosmatose's *Leviathan* and James Cameron's *The Abyss*. Burg contributed to several of Cameron's subsequent projects (*Terminator 2*, *T2-3D: Battle Across Time*), as well as Paul Verhoeven's *Total Recall* and *Starship Troopers*, Kevin Costner's *Dances With Wolves* and *Waterworld*, Robert Zemeckis' *Contact*, and David Twohy's *The Chronicles of Riddick*. He is well-established as a designer-illustrator with extensive credits in entertainment design.

Burg is currently engaged at Electronic Arts' Los Angeles studio, where he crafts visuals for next-generation console games.

Self-taught in traditional illustration, Burg has embraced digital media. He lives in Pasadena, California, and strives to further his development as an artist while keeping a busy professional schedule.

E-mail: spBurg@pacbell.net

JAMES CLYNE

James Clyne attended the University of California at Santa Barbara where he studied fine art and painting. Eager to concentrate on design, he attended Art Center College of Design as an industrial design major, focusing on entertainment design. Clyne began his professional career designing creatures, characters, and environments for gaming companies such as Sega, Activision, and Pulse Entertainment. Wanting to further expand his work in entertainment design, Clyne began consulting as a concept artist and storyboard artist for special effects houses such as Digital Domain and Rhythm & Hues. His early work in film began with *Fear and Loathing in Las Vegas*. Following were *Instinct*, *Titan A.E.*, *Mission to Mars*, *Galaxy Quest*, *Mystery Men*, *Artificial Intelligence: A.I.*, *Minority Report*, *The Polar Express*, and *Troy*, for which he provided conceptual design for environments, sets, props, matte paintings, and vehicles.

Web site: www.JamesClyne.com
E-mail: Clyne@ix.netcom.com

MARK GOERNER

Mark Goerner is one of L.A.'s leading concept artists, and has done design content and illustration work for the television, film, automotive, theme park, and gaming industries. Goerner graduated from Art Center College of Design in 1996 with distinction in transportation design and an emphasis on entertainment design. Since then he has worked with BMW/Designworks, Coca-Cola, Rhythm & Hues for Disney, Kraft, Honda, and Intel, along with other local and international companies. His current focus is designing architectural spaces, props, transportation, and characters for such films as *Minority Report*, *Constantine*, *X2: X-Men United*, *Superman Returns*, and *The Terminal*.

Web site: www.GRNR.com
E-mail: Mark@GRNR.com

NEVILLE PAGE

Neville Page was educated at Art Center College of Design in Pasadena California. Although his major was product design, he has always gravitated towards entertainment. With the combination of his education and personal interest, Neville has found himself involved with quite a variety of projects from creature design and sculpture to conceptual design and engineering. His clients have included Universal Studios, Warner Bros., 20th Century Fox, Mattel, and BMW to name just a few. He is currently involved with the new film project *The Chronicles of Narnia: The Lion, The Witch and the Wardrobe*. Neville has also taught at Art Center College of Design (Pasadena and Switzerland), Otis College, Gnomon and corporate workshops.

Web site: www.NevillePage.com
E-mail: NevPage@aol.com

NICK PUGH

Concept designer Nick Pugh gravitates to creative challenges. He has been pursuing originality in the fields of vehicle and entertainment design for over 15 years. Nick works as a lead concept artist for the visual effects studio Rhythm & Hues, where he creates original character, vehicle, FX, and production design for feature films, commercials, and print. Recent film credits include *The Chronicles of Narnia: The Lion, The Witch and The Wardrobe*, *Skeleton Key*, *Serenity*, *The Ring 2*, and *Garfield*. He also designs and builds unique concept cars that explore the limits of what is possible. His work can often be seen in books and media publications.

Web site: www.NickPugh.com
E-mail: Nick@NickPugh.com

SCOTT ROBERTSON

Scott Robertson is a concept designer, teacher, and publisher. After graduating from Art Center College of Design with honors in Transportation Design, Scott opened a product design consulting firm in San Francisco with Neville Page. Some of their clients included Kestrel, Giro Sport Design, Nissan, Volvo and Yamaha. Five years later, he relocated to Vevey, Switzerland to teach drawing and industrial design at Art Center, Europe. Now based in Los Angeles, Scott teaches at Art Center College of Design and has developed the curriculum for a new Entertainment Design program. Scott recently art directed Mattel's Hot Wheels AcceleRacers collectible card game, designed a Hot Wheels car, and authored *How To Draw Cars The Hot Wheels Way*. Dedicated to art and education, Scott founded the publishing company, Design Studio Press, with nine books currently in print.

Web site: www.DrawThrough.com
E-mail: Scott@DrawThrough.com

NICOLAS BOUVIER

Sparth, the artistic alter ego of Nicolas Bouvier, has been an active concept designer in the gaming industry since 1995. He has participated, as artistic director and concept designer, in several major game licenses such as *Prince of Persia* and *Alone in the Dark*. He has also contributed to a large number of book covers for the French market, illustrating Frank Herbert's *Dune* saga, as well as several novels from Jack Vance and Robert Heinlein.

Sparth has travelled extensively from an early age, living in the United States, Singapore, China, France, and Europe. He has been influenced by many cultures, observed people, and wrote down the details. He is passionate about space, buildings, and robotics, but one of his greatest passions is contemporary architecture, whose principles he experiments with in his own art.

Sparth currently lives in Montreal, Canada, where he works with the gaming companys Darkworks Studio and Ubisoft Montreal.

Web site: www.Sparth.com
E-mail: nbSparth@gmail.com

RYAN CHURCH

Ryan Church has worked as a concept designer or illustrator with every major Hollywood film studio, Industrial Light and Magic, and Lucasfilm. For the last four years, Church was both senior art director at ILM and concept design supervisor at Skywalker Ranch, where he worked on *Star Wars: Episodes II* and *III* from the earliest concept ideation through to art direction, approval of final shots, and the movies' final look. His favorite part of the job is the rough early-concept stage, but his work is most visible in the way his concepts and compositions make it through to the final frame.

Web site: www.RyanChurch.com
E-mail: RyanChurch@earthlink.net

DYLAN COLE

California-native Dylan Cole graduated from the University of California, Los Angeles with a degree in fine art. Originally intending to be a comic book artist or book cover illustrator, he turned to matte painting instead. After a brief stint at Illusion Arts on *The Time Machine*, smaller jobs led to him working at Rhythm & Hues on *Daredevil*. Cole then moved to New Zealand for a year to be a senior matte painter on *The Lord of The Rings: Return of the King* for Weta.

He later returned to R&H as lead matte painter on *The Chronicles of Riddick*. Recent credits include *I, Robot*, *Van Helsing*, *Sky Captain and the World of Tomorrow*, and *The Aviator*. He was also visual effects art director on *The Ring 2*. Cole is currently venturing into concept work for video games while continuing to do matte painting for such films as *The Chronicles of Narnia: The Lion, The Witch, and The Wardrobe* and *Memoirs of a Geisha*. He also recently finished a series of DVDs for The Gnomon Workshop on matte painting.

Web site: www.DylanColeStudio.com
E-mail: Dylan@DylanColeStudio.com

KASRA FARAHANI

Kasra Farahani is a Los Angeles-based artist and designer. He studied industrial design at the Art Center College of Design in Pasadena, California, and has consulted in product design, furniture design, game design, theme park design, and film design. Kasra began production designing independent films while attending Art Center, and continues to do so now while working as a conceptual illustrator on large-scale productions. His recent feature credits include *Team America: World Police*, *Bewitched*, *War of the Worlds*, *Jarhead*, and *Miami Vice*.

Web site: www.Zafron.com
E-mail: Kasra@zafron.com

SEAN HARGREAVES

Blackpool, England-native Sean Hargreaves attended Art Center College of Design, where he graduated with a B.S. After school, Hargreaves worked at General Motors Advanced Concepts Center where he designed concept cars. But a lifelong interest in films—as well as in architecture, transportation design, and art—drew him to the entertainment industry, where he worked his way up from storyboard artist, concept artist, and art director to production designer. Hargreaves now oversees the design and construction of sets for commercials and films. He has worked on such films as *Heat*, *Crimson Tide*, *Batman Forever*, *Seven*, and *The Lost World: Jurassic Park*, and has won two AICP awards for production design. Two of his commercials are in The Museum of Modern Art in New York.

Web site: www.SeanHargreavesDesign.com
E-mail: Sean@SeanHargreavesDesign.com

KHANG LE

Khang Le was born in Saigon, Vietnam, in 1981. When he was ten, his family moved to Los Angeles, California, and Le immersed himself in the world of comic books. During high school, a friend introduced him to Art Center College of Design in Pasadena. At the same time, *The Art of Star Wars, Episode I: The Phantom Menace* came out, solidifying Le's aspiration to become a concept artist for the entertainment industry. In 2000, he was accepted to ACCD, where he refined his skills and freelanced for various entertainment media, including games, movies, music videos, and publishing. He has recently graduated and is currently traveling the world and considering all of his professional options.

Web site: www.KhangLe.net
E-mail: KhangLe81@yahoo.com

WARREN MANSER

Warren Manser is a freelance conceptual artist living in Los Angeles, California. He has primarily worked in the film industry, but has also had the opportunity to be involved with theme park design, video games, animation, as well as other creative industries. Manser is originally from Detroit, Michigan, where he studied industrial design at the Center for Creative Studies. As an intern for Ford Motor Company, he designed the exterior of the "Splash" concept car. After finishing college, Warren decided to relocate to Los Angeles, where he's had the opportunity work on a variety of artistically and creatively challenging projects such as *Army of Darkness*, *The Matrix*, *Pearl Harbor*, and *Spider-Man*.

Web site: www.WarrenManser.com
E-mail: wcManser@mac.com

STEPHAN MARTINIERE

Stephan Martiniere is an internationally renowned science fiction and fantasy artist. He is the recipient of numerous awards including a silver and a gold Spectrum award and three gold and six silver Exposé awards. Martiniere has worked in various fields of endeavor such as animation, video games, theme parks, and book covers. He is also an accomplished concept artist who has worked on movies such as *I, Robot*, *Star Wars: Episodes II & III*, *Virus*, *Red Planet*, *Sphere*, *Titan A.E.*, and *The Time Machine*. As a visual design director for Cyan, Martiniere was responsible for creating and overseeing the look of the game *URU: Ages Beyond Myst*, its two expansion packs, and *Myst 5*.

Martiniere has created a book of his sci-fi book covers and personal art for Design Studio Press called *Quantum Dreams: The Art of Stephan Martiniere*. He is currently the visual design director for Midway games in Chicago.

Web site: www.Martiniere.com
E-mail: Martiniere@comcast.net

ED NATIVIDAD

Ed Natividad studied transportation design in Detroit, Michigan. An internship at GM's Advanced Concept Center in Thousand Oaks, California, brought him to the West Coast, where he saw the potential for designing in film. He returned to Detroit to finish his final semesters, but took issue with the school's required curriculum. Ultimately, he was expelled from school for reasons not known, ensuring that he would not work in the automotive industry any time soon. Jumping in a car and driving west for three days without a safety net was not necessarily a bad thing. It wasn't as easy as Natividad thought either. He now works in the film industry on various productions such as *Star Wars: Episodes I & II*, *Terminator 3: Rise of the Machines*, and *I, Robot*.

E-mail: EdNatividad@comcast.net

RICK O'BRIEN

As one of two sons in an Air Force family, Rick O'Brien spent his earliest years stationed at various bases with brief stints in South Carolina, Taiwan, Illinois, and finally to the deserts of Arizona. Discovering art his sophomore year of college, O'Brien ultimately graduated with a B.F.A. from the University of Arizona in Tucson. A flirtation with illustration was the prelude to a life-altering voyage to Ireland and the Czech Republic, where he experienced first-hand the aesthetics that would come to inform his later work—cobblestone, wood, plaster, damp air, and pivo, or beer.

In spring 1998, O'Brien moved to Los Angeles. He has since served in various production and art departments for the entertainment industry, working as a set and property builder, designer, sculptor, toy maker, and carpenter. His more recent preoccupation visits an old passion—paint. O'Brien lives in Eagle Rock, California where he is working on an upcoming book of personal art.

Web site: www.TheMonumentProject.com
E-mail: RickOBrien.tmp@earthlink.net

DAN QUARNSTROM

One of Rhythm & Hues' premier art directors, Dan Quarnstrom's experience spans decades and a wide range of disciplines, from illustration and traditional 2-D animation to computer-generated 3-D animation. Starting as an illustrator and designer, Quarnstrom's early career involved freelance work for magazines, record labels, and advertising. He joined the pioneering motion-graphics firm Robert Abel and Associates in the 1970s, where the emerging technology of computer-generated imagery was being developed and applied to commercials and films. He later followed fellow Abel alumnus John Hughes and partners to their new venture, Rhythm & Hues Studios. Today, Quarnstrom contributes to visual development for films and commercials. He has directed spots for Coca-Cola and Kodak, and contributes to the character design process of countless R&H projects. He recently participated in a group "car culture" show at the Mendenhall-Sobieski gallery in Pasadena, along with Robert Williams and Big Daddy Roth.

E-mail: 3dq@comcast.net

CHRISTIAN L. SCHEURER

Christian Lorenz Scheurer was born in Switzerland and received his M.F.A. at St. Luc Art Academy in Brussels, Belgium. He won the prestigious Philip Morris Award for his graphic novels and worked on movies and award-winning commercials in Europe before moving to Hollywood. During his U.S. career, Christian has worked on some of the most innovative movies, games, and commercials in the entertainment industry as a conceptual designer, matte painter, and art director. His high-profile film resume includes *The Fifth Element*, *Titanic*, *Dark City*, *What Dreams May Come*, *The Matrix*, *Final Fantasy*, *Animatrix: The Final Flight of the Osiris*, and *The Day After Tomorrow*. His game credits include *Final Fantasy IX*, *Lord of the Rings: Return of the King* (art director) and *Spore* (conceptual art director). Currently, Scheurer serves as a visual consultant to prominent industry leaders, helping to shape the direction of next-generation feature films and video games.

Web site: www.ChristianLorenzScheurer.com
E-mail: cScheurer@earthlink.net

OLIVER SCHOLL

German-born Oliver Scholl was a published artist by age 15, and later studied industrial design. Inked cross-section drawings of spaceships evolved over time to full-color work for publishing and advertising agencies in his home country. Conceptual design work for German director Roland Emmerich led to Scholl's transition into the motion picture industry and his relocation in 1991 to Los Angeles. He is most noted for the production design of *The Time Machine*, *Godzilla*, and *Independence Day (ID4)*. Scholl also worked as conceptual designer or illustrator on such feature films as *Stargate*, *Batman Forever*, *Titan A.E.*, *The Haunting*, *Mission to Mars*, *Artificial Intelligence: A.I.*, *The Polar Express*, and *Stealth*, as well as several TV pilots. In addition to doing work for themed entertainment and commercials, Scholl has recently created cover artwork for over 20 new publications by VPM and Heyne-Random House, Germany.

Web site: www.OliverScholl.com
E-mail: os@OliverScholl.com

FARZAD VARAHRAMYAN

Farzad Varahramyan received a B.F.A. from the University of Alberta, Canada, and a B.S. with honors from Art Center College of Design, majoring in product design. He has been a video game developer for the last ten years, and has also contributed designs on such films as *Jumanji*, and most recently *Alien Vs. Predator*. In 2002, Varahramyan was asked to be cofounder and a director at High Moon Studios, establishing their concept art department and helping to develop the visual DNA for all the games at the studio. He attributes his good fortune in concept art to his teachers and mentors such as Andy Ogden, Richard Pietruska, Norman Schureman, Joe Farrer, Gary Meyer, Warren Manser, Lorne Lanning, Steven Olds, and the talented artists he works with every day. However, the biggest influences in his life have been his wife Vera, son Maxwell, and daughter Isabella.

E-mail: info@FarzadArt.com

MIKE YAMADA

Michael Yamada was born and raised in Pasadena, California. He wanted to be a graphic designer, but changed his course of study at his local community college after discovering a book of *Star Wars* production art. He then transferred to Art Center College of Design where in 2003 he graduated with honors with a B.S. degree in product design with an emphasis on entertainment design. Since graduation, he has worked as a visual development artist at DreamWorks Animation, contributing to a variety of freelance projects. He also teaches at Otis College of Art and Design.

Web site: www.mYamada.com
E-mail: Mike@mYamada.com

FELIX YOON

Felix Yoon was born in Pennsylvania in 1982. He spent his childhood there, and later relocated to South Korea. He moved to California as he entered high school, and it wasn't until senior year that Yoon decided to take art seriously as a possible occupation. After high school he entered Art Center College of Design, where he graduated with honors with a B.F.A. in illustration. Yoon is one of three Art Center students who created *The Skillful Huntsman* (Design Studio Press, 2005).

Yoon started working as a concept artist for video games and now works as a visual development artist at DreamWorks Animation.

E-mail: FelixYoon@hotmail.com

FENG ZHU

Zhu studied industrial design at the Art Center College of Design. Under his own studio, Feng Zhu Design, he has worked on a diverse array of projects including video games, TV commercials, film design, and amusement park rides. Some of his clients include Lucasfilm, Disney, Blur Studio, Electronic Arts, Digital Extremes, Epic Games, Microsoft, Film Roman, Universal, Warner Brothers, ROBOT, and Sierra. He has recently worked with director James Cameron (*Titanic*) on his next film, as well as director Michael Bay (*Pearl Harbor*) for his 2005 movie *The Island*.

Feng Zhu Design, along with DSP and The Gnomon Workshop, has produced the first ever analog training DVDs. Zhu's studio is currently producing his own line of toys and collectables. Zhu is also the cofounder of Gamma Ray Studios, along with his partner James Clyne.

Web site: www.ArtByFeng.com
E-mail: FenZhu@yahoo.com

artist: Mark Goerner
title: REEF CITY
media: digital
size: 3082 x 4500 pixels
page: 9

artist: Mark Goerner
title: LORD REGINALD THE 7TH
media: digital
size: 2850 x 4000 pixels
page: 11

artist: Mark Goerner
title: PILE O' FODDER
media: pen
size: various
page: 13

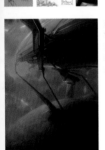

artist: Mark Goerner
title: GIGABOCCE
media: digital
size: 3213 x 4500 pixels
page: 15

artist: Mark Goerner
title: NEO ROME
media: digital
size: 5000 x 2615 pixels
page: 17

artist: Mark Goerner
title: GRAND CENTRAL
media: digital
size: 5000 x 2630 pixels
page: 18

artist: Mark Goerner
title: HOUSE ALLUVIAL
media: mixed
size: 8.25 x 11.25 inches
page: 21

artist: Mark Goerner
title: NOCTURNAL TRANSMISSION
media: digital
size: 3300 x 4200 pixels
page: 23

artist: Mark Goerner
title: VERNAL REPRISE
media: digital
size: 5000 x 2850 pixels
page: 25

artist: Mark Goerner
title: CRIMSON CRAFT
media: digital
size: 3500 x 2000 pixels
page: 26

artist: Nick Pugh
title: TROPICAL CREATURE
media: digital
size: 2992 x 4080 pixels
page: 29

artist: Nick Pugh
title: BARNYARD
media: mixed
size: 2992 x 4080 pixels
page: 31

artist: Nick Pugh
title: 15 KINGSBURY
media: digital
size: 2360 X 2700 pixels
page: 33

artist: Nick Pugh
title: SEA CREATURE
media: digital
size: 2300 X 2792 pixels
page: 34

artist: Nick Pugh
title: BABISON
media: digital
size: 3032 X 3900 pixels
page: 34

artist: Nick Pugh
title: VEHICLES
media: digital
size: 3032 X 3900 pixels
page: 36

artist: Nick Pugh
title: VEHICLES
media: digital
size:
page: 37

artist: Nick Pugh
title: VEHICLES
media: digital
size: 4020 x 5040 pixels
page: 39

artist: Nick Pugh
title: SCULPTURE
media: sculpy
size: 6 inches tall
page: 46

artist: Nick Pugh
title: SCULPTURE
media: sculpy
size: 30 inches tall
page: 47

artist: Scott Robertson
title: LAUNCH CRANE
media: digital
size: 3966 x 5272 pixels
page: 49

artist: Scott Robertson
title: ANT SHIPS
media: graphite
size: 9 x 9 inches
page: 50

artist: Scott Robertson
title: ASCENT
media: digital
size: 3875 x 2885 pixels
page: 52

artist: Scott Robertson
title: CHECK POINT 12
media: digital
size: 3300 x 4480 pixels
page: 53

artist: Scott Robertson
title: SPACE SHIPS
media: chisel point pen
size: 9 x 9 inches
page: 54

artist: Scott Robertson
title: THE LANDING
media: digital
size: 5117 x 2384 pixels
page: 57

artist: Scott Robertson
title: PURPLE BRAIN
media: digital
size: 3875 x 2597 pixels
page: 60

artist: Scott Robertson
title: LEAF CITY, REPAIRS, LAB
media: digital
size: various
page: 61

artist: Scott Robertson
title: CRAWLER ISLAND
media: digital
size: 4536 x 2760, 4536 x 1920 pixels
page: 63

artist: James Clyne
title: VENUS NOIR
media: digital
size: 4950 x 2991 pixels
page: 81

artist: Steve Burg
title: CATACOMB III: AIRLIFT
media: digital
size: 4950 x 3375 pixels
page: 97

artist: James Clyne
title: CYPRESS CITY
media: digital
size: 4950 x 2992 pixels
page: 82

artist: Steve Burg
title: ARCOLOGY I: ASCENDANT
media: digital
size: 5016 x 2820 pixels
page: 98

artist: Scott Robertson
title: RANDOM STARTS
media: digital
size: 300 dpi
page: 66

artist: James Clyne
title: CHUPACABRA
media: prismacolor
size: 9 x 9 inches
page: 84

artist: Steve Burg
title: ARCOLOGY II: THE FALL
media: digital
size: 2475 x 3375 pixels
page: 100

artist: James Clyne
title: SELF-PORTRAIT
media: digital
size: 2475 x 3153 pixels
page: 69

artist: James Clyne
title: CHUPACABRA
media: prismacolor
size: 9 x 12 inches
page: 85

artist: Steve Burg
title: ARCOLOGY II: THE FALL
media: digital
size: 2475 x 3375 pixels
page: 101

artist: James Clyne
title: A SLIVER OF HOPE
media: digital
size: 2386 x 3375 pixels
page: 71

artist: James Clyne
title: LOS ANGELES
media: digital
size: 2475 x 3375 pixels
page: 87

artist: Steve Burg
title: ARCOLOGY III: MONUMENT
media: digital
size: 2475 x 3375 pixels
page: 103

artist: James Clyne
title: HARWA MARKETPLACE
media: digital
size: 3450 x 2076 pixels
page: 73

artist: Steve Burg
title: VISITORS
media: digital
size: 300 dpi
page: 89

artist: Steve Burg
title: BEHEMOTH
media: digital
size: 2475 x 3375 pixels
page: 105

artist: James Clyne
title: QUANTUM FETISH
media: digital
size: 4950 x 2100 pixels
page: 74

artist: James Clyne
title: A JOURNEY WITH HIS DONKEY
media: acrylic
size: 2184 x 2592 pixels
page: 76

artist: Steve Burg
title: CITADEL
media: digital
size: 2475 x 3375 pixels
page: 91

artist: Steve Burg
title: SIGHTING
media: digital
size: 2475 x 3375 pixels
page: 107

artist: James Clyne
title: A JOURNEY WITH HIS DONKEY
media: digital
size: 2399 x 3375 pixels
page: 77

artist: Steve Burg
title: CATACOMB I: SPHINX
media: digital
size: 2475 x 3375 pixels
page: 93

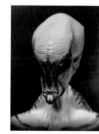

artist: Steve Burg
title: CATACOMB II: PROCESSING PLANT
media: digital
size: 2475 x 3375 pixels
page: 95

artist: James Clyne
title: THE TRASHBIN
media: digital
size: 1616 x 673, 1605 x 1735 pixels
page: 79

artist: Neville Page
title: ALIEN HEAD
media: digital
size: 3222 x 4308 pixels
page: 109

artist: Neville Page
title: CAUDAL LURING
media: prismacolor
size: 14 x 17 inches each
page: 111

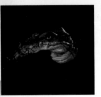

artist: Neville Page
title: CAUDAL LURING 2
media: sculpy
size: 8 inches long
page: 112

artist: Neville Page
title: MISCELLANEOUS ANIMALS 2
media: prismacolor
size: 14 x 17 inches each
page: 115

artist: Neville Page
title: MOUTHY
media: digital
size: 3270 x 3708 pixels
page: 119

artist: Neville Page
title: OLD MAN
media: digital
size: 3300 x 4500 pixels
page: 121

artist: Neville Page
title: SNAIL MALE
media: digital
size: various
page: 122

artist: Neville Page
title: SNAIL MALE
media: prismacolor
size: 14 x 17 inches
page: 123

artist: Neville Page
title: TREE HUGGER
media: wed clay
size: 20 inches long
page: 125

artist: Neville Page
title: WILDER BEAST
media: digital
size: 3300 x 1920 pixels
page: 127

artist: Harald Belker
title: HB-R
media: digital
size: 4950 x 3375
page: 129

artist: Harald Belker
title: CORVETTE: LEVITATION STYLE
media: digital
size: 4950 x 3375
page: 130

artist: Harald Belker
title: 911
media: digital
size: 2475 x 3375
page: 133

artist: Harald Belker
title: BUSTED
media: digital
size: 2475 x 3375
page: 135

artist: Harald Belker
title: DVD TUTORIAL
media: digital
size: 4950 x 3375
page: 137

artist: Harald Belker
title: SILVER METALLIC
media: digital
size: 7764 x 3384
page: 138-139

artist: Harald Belker
title: CHROME SLED
media: digital
size: 2475 x 3375
page: 141

artist: Harald Belker
title: HB-X
media: digital and prismacolor
size: 2475 x 3375
page: 143

artist: Harald Belker
title: MACHINES
media: digital
size: 2325 x 2175
page: 144

artist: Harald Belker
title: MACHINES
media: digital
size: 2475 x 3375
page: 145

artist: Harald Belker
title: WAR PLANE
media: digital
size: 2475 x 3375
page: 147

artist: Sparth (Nicolas Bouvier)
title: CARAPACES
media: digital
size: 2230 x 1150, 1900 x 985 pixels
page: 150

artist: Sparth (Nicolas Bouvier)
title: CARAPACES
media: digital
size: various
page: 151

artist: Ryan Church
title: DRIVE-THRU, FISHING
media: digital
size: 1550 x 614, 5038 x 1858 pixels
page: 152

artist: Ryan Church
title: BALLOON BEASTS
media: digital
size: 4164 x 7313 pixels
page: 153

artist: Dylan Cole
title: CITIES
media: digital
size: various
page: 154

artist: Dylan Cole
title: CITIES
media: digital
size: 4096 x 2035, 4096 x 2134 pixels
page: 155

artist: Kasra Farahani
title: Excerpts from NOON
media: digital
size: 3084 x 1667 pixels
page: 156

artist: Kasra Farahani
title: Excerpts from NOON
media: digital
size: 3084 x 1667, 3632 x 1963 pixels
page: 157

artist: Sean Hargreaves
title: MAS DECOSTIJL
media: digital
size: various
page: 158

artist: Sean Hargreaves
title: MAS DECOSTIJL
media: digital
size: various
page: 159

artist: Khang Le
title: PARKING STRUCTURE
media: graphite
size: 7.75 x 7.25 inches
page: 160

artist: Khang Le
title: PARKING STRUCTURE
media: digital
size: 2475 x 3375 pixels
page: 161

artist: Ed Natividad
title: ANATOMICAL VEHICLES
media: mixed
size: 7.75 x 7.25 inches
page: 162

artist: Ed Natividad
title: ANATOMICAL VEHICLES
media: mixed
size: 8.25 x 11.25 inches
page: 163

artist: Warren Manser
title: Excerpts From
        CONSTELLATION ORION
media: mixed
size: 2325 x 2175 pixels
page: 164

artist: Warren Manser
title: Excerpts From
        CONSTELLATION ORION
media: mixed
size: 3300 x 1932, 3300 x 2070 pixels
page: 165

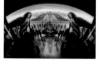

artist: Stephan Martiniere
title: NAUTILUS (detail)
media: digital
size: 2325 x 2175 pixels
page: 166

artist: Stephan Martiniere
title: NAUTILUS
media: digital
size: 2475 x 3375 pixels
page: 167

artist: Rick O'Brien
title: THE RANGE OF HUMANITY
media: oil
size: 24 x 48 inches
page: 168

artist: Rick O'Brien
title: THE RANGE OF HUMANITY
media: oil
size: 24 x 48 inches
page: 169

artist: Dan Quarnstrom
title: JOYRIDE
media: mixed
size: Post-It sized
page: 170

artist: Dan Quarnstrom
title: FLATOUT
media: ink
size: various
page: 171

artist: Christian Lorenz Scheurer
title: PROCESSION OF EFFIGIES
media: mixed
size: various
page: 172

artist: Christian Lorenz Scheurer
title: PROCESSION OF EFFIGIES
media: digital
size: 4950 x 6543 pixels
page: 173

artist: Oliver Scholl
title: SEEDS
media: digital
size: 2325 x 2175 pixels
page: 174

artist: Oliver Scholl
title: SEEDS
media: digital
size: 2475 x 3375 pixels
page: 175

artist: Farzad Varahramyan
title: MECHBETH
media: prismacolor and ink
size: various
page: 176

artist: Farzad Varahramyan
title: MECHBETH
media: digital
size: 2321 x 3375 pixels
page: 177

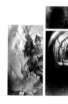

artist: Mike Yamada
title: SKETCHES
media: graphite
size: various
page: 178

artist: Mike Yamada
title: SKETCHES
media: graphite
size: various
page: 179

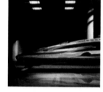

artist: Felix Yoon
title: REST STOP
media: digital
size: 2328 x 2175 pixels
page: 180

artist: Felix Yoon
title: FLIGHT
media: digital
size: 1650 x 2250 pixels
page: 181

artist: Feng Zhu
title: TEMPLE, CHARGE
media: digital
size: 3200 x 1358 pixels each
page: 182

artist: Feng Zhu
title: NEW EMPIRE
media: digital
size: 2551 x 3400 pixels
page: 183

other titles by Titan Books:

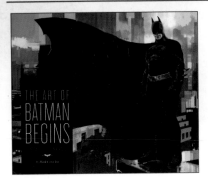

ISBN 1 84576 094 8

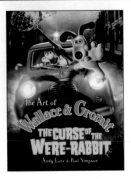

ISBN 1 84576 215 0

ISBN 1 84576 004 2

ISBN 1 84023 882 8 hardback
ISBN 1 84023 941 7 paperback

ISBN 1 84576 286 X

ISBN 1 85286 926 7

ISBN 1 84023 893 3

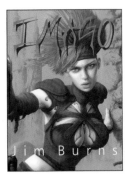

ISBN 1 84576 133 2

educational DVDs by design studio press and the gnomon workshop:

Creature Design Illustration
Form Language Refinement
with Nick Pugh

Harald Belker
Vol. 1: Intro to Car Design & Drawing
Vol. 2: Digital Automotive Rendering
Vol. 3: Integrating a Vehicle
Vol. 4: Car Design & Presentation
Vol. 5: Movie Prop Design & Presentation

Ryan Church
Vol. 1: Rendering Matte Vehicles
Vol. 2: Rendering Shiny Vehicles
Vol. 3: High-Tech Architecture
Vol. 4: Low-Tech Architecture
Vol. 5: Architectural Interior

James Clyne
Vol. 1: Environmental Sketching & Design
Vol. 2: Rendering a Cinematic Environment

Dylan Cole
Intro to Landscape Matte Painting
Intro to Cityscape Matte Painting
Advanced Digital Matte Painting

Mark Goerner
Vol. 1: Sketching Interior Spaces
Vol. 2: Rendering Interior Spaces

Neville Page
Vol. 1: Character Design-Fantasy Wildebeest
Vol. 2: Digital Painting-Fantasy Wildebeest
Vol. 3: Rendering Eyes
Vol. 4: Rendering Flesh

Nick Pugh
Originality in Design
Creature Design Illustration
Creature & Environment Rendering

Scott Robertson
Vol. 1: Basic Perspective Form Drawing
Vol. 2: How to Draw Cars
Vol. 3: How to Draw Aircraft
Vol. 4: How to Draw Hovercraft & Spacecraft
Creating Unique Environments
Industrial Design Rendering-Bicycle

Christian Scheurer
Intro to Digital Painting in Adobe Photoshop
Advanced Digital Painting in Adobe Photoshop

Feng Zhu
Vol. 1: Design Process-Fighting Robots
Vol. 2: Robot Refinement & Rendering
Vol. 3: The Fundamentals of Shot Design for Environments
CD 1: Vehicle Sketching
CD 2: Environments
CD 3: Quick Sketching
CD 4: Digital Painting

To order copies of the DVDs and to view other DVDs we offer, please visit: **www.thegnomonworkshop.com** or write to: Design Studio Press, 8577 Higuera Street, Culver City, CA 90232, USA
tel: 001.310.836.3116 fax: 001.310.836.1136

TITAN BOOKS

Did you enjoy this book? We love to hear from our readers.
Please email us at: **readerfeedback@titanemail.com**
or write to **Reader Feedback** at Titan Books' address.

To receive advance information, news, competitions, and exclusive Titan offers online, please register as a member by clicking the "sign up" button on our website: **www.titanbooks.com**

Titan Books are available from all good bookshops, or visit our website: **www.titanbooks.com**